Common Sense, Uncommon

4 Secrets of HIGH Performing Organizations

OTHER BOOKS
BY BUD BILANICH

Supervisory Leadership and the New Factory:
Getting Extraordinary Things Done
on the Shop Floor

Using Values to Turn Vision
into Reality

Four Secrets of
High Performing Organizations

"An elegantly simple but complete explanation of the best principles of leadership. This book serves as a reminder of the power and importance of doing the basics well. It belongs in the ready reference section of any thoughtful manager."

Karen Katen, Executive Vice President, Pfizer Inc;
President, Pfizer Global Pharmaceuticals

"Simple but powerful concepts come to life in this very readable book. Anyone interested in creating a high performing organization will benefit from the ideas in it."

Chase Carey, Chairman and CEO, Fox Television Group

"This book is jampacked with useful, real-world information. It pinpoints the importance of moving beyond mere good intentions to action. Bud Bilanich has given business people everywhere a model for true success. Buy it, read it, USE IT!"

Eric Harvey, President of the Walk the Talk Company
and author of the popular Walk the Talk *book series*

"Bud Bilanich does a great job of explaining the complexities of business in the 21st century and in offering a simple, easy-to-use set of ideas any leader can use to create a high performing organization."

Lee Bolman and Terry Deal, co-authors, Leading with Soul

"I loved this little book. It was fun to read and made me think. It thrusts the reader into the mind of a CEO and shows what it takes to create and maintain a high performing organization. I'm buying a copy for all of my clients."

Jack Davis, Partner, Dot Com Advisors

"For family businesses and their multiple organizational challenges, Bud Bilanich's book presents an educational yet entertaining tool to address and implement the fundamental principles of organizational success."

Francois M. de Visscher, President, de Visscher & Co.;
Past President, Family Firm Institute

"This little book dispenses the type of common-sense wisdom all too often lacking in business school curriculums."

Norman Bartczak, Ph.D., Columbia Graduate School of
Business Administration

"A great story full of wisdom that applies to leaders of all types of organizations, regardless of mission. I've made a wallet-sized card of the four secrets and use them in my day-to-day work. Clarity, commitment, execution and relationships work for me."

John Arigoni, President and CEO,
Boys and Girls Clubs of Metro Denver

"At first glance, the ideas in *Four Secrets of High Performing Organizations* seem like common sense. However, this is a book of uncommon wisdom. Bud Bilanich has done a good job of blending his real-world, practical experience with his storytelling skills to create an outstanding illustration of what it takes to succeed in today's ever-changing, highly complex business environment."

Don Nelson, Senior VP Human Resources, Pfizer Inc

"This practical book is for leaders interested in increasing the performance of their organizations. Any leader, from the CEO to the mail room supervisor, will find useful, easy-to-implement ideas in this book."

Ron Guziak, Executive Director, Hoag Hospital Foundation,
Newport Beach, CA

4 Secrets of HIGH Performing Organizations

Beyond the Flavor of the Month
to Lasting Results

BUD BILANICH

FRONT ROW PRESS

875 S. Colorado Blvd., #773 • Denver, CO 80246 • 303.393.0446

Published by Front Row Press
875 S. Colorado Blvd., #773
Denver, CO 80246
(303) 393-0446

ISBN 1-929774-13-3
Library of Congress Control Number: 2002104694

Jacket Design and Book Interior:
Benson Communications
Denver, Colorado
www.bensoncomm.com

Copies of *Four Secrets of High Performing Organizations* are available in bookstores everywhere and through Front Row Press.
Call (303) 393-0446 or order online at www.oegconsulting.com

DEDICATED TO

Brennan Frederick Newell

1974 - 2000

"Free as a bird now . . ."

· ACKNOWLEDGEMENTS ·

Writing a book is not easy. Attempting to thank all the people who have helped make this book possible is almost as difficult. First, I'd like to thank Cathy, my wonderful wife. Without her, I could never manage my difficult travel, consulting and writing schedule.

Over the years I've had the good fortune of working with many people who have provided me with the insight I needed to write this book. Tony Maddaluna, Nat Ricciardi, Jay Cayado, Rich Illingworth, Don Nelson, Gordon Borteck, Howard Sohn, Steve Roesler, Van Horsley, Maggie Watson and Tim Beever are all excellent leaders who will undoubtedly recognize some of their ideas in the pages of this book.

John Guaspari, another consultant and friend, introduced me to the value equation on page 138. I got the fad-surfing idea from Eileen Shapiro's excellent book *Fad Surfing in the Boardroom.* Similarly, Geary Rummler's book *Improving Performance: How to Manage the White Space on the Organization Chart* inspired my comments on white-space management. Finally, when I was a student at Harvard, Lee Bolman and Terry Deal introduced me to the importance of multiple perspectives for understanding and leading organizations. Their course inspired the original idea for this book.

· ACKNOWLEDGEMENTS ·

Several of my friends and colleagues read and commented on the manuscript. Warren Mersereau, Don Kirkpatrick, Bob Barton and I spent several hours discussing everything about the book, from its content to its design. Thanks guys, I owe you! John Arigoni, Stephanie Warakomski, Grace Larson, Bill McNeill, Bob Donovan, Buzz Murphy, Tom Booth, Angelo Santisi, Donna Degutis, Sally Simpson, Mitch Marks, Dianne Harri, Ron Pantello, Betsy Blee, Mark Morgan and Lori Hansen all read and commented on the manuscript. Their input was invaluable.

Deb Hvass, my editor, did an excellent job of making my prose more readable and concise. Bobbi Benson, artist extraordinaire, did a great job in designing both the book and its cover. Paul Abdoo gets the credit for the cover photo.

My deepest thanks to all those mentioned above — and to anyone I may have missed.

I read Stephen King's book, *On Writing* when I was writing this book. While my work is no *Carrie* or *The Shining,* it's a lot better because of his clear and helpful advice.

BY ERIC HARVEY

One of the fun things about writing a book is that you get to meet a lot of interesting people once the book is published. After *Walk the Talk* was published, Bud Bilanich was one of the most interesting people Al Lucia and I had the good fortune to meet. Bud called us after he read our book. He said that he liked our ideas and wanted to discuss them further. He flew to Dallas one day about eight years ago to talk about the relationship between organizational values and high performance. That meeting marked the beginning of an interesting and rewarding professional and personal relationship between Bud and me.

Four Secrets of High Performing Organizations is Bud's third book. Like the other two, it is full of practical wisdom presented in an entertaining, easy-to-read, down-to-earth manner. Bud shares my belief that simple is better than complex. His books reflect his ability to grapple with complex concepts and present them in an easily understandable manner.

This book tells the story of Diamond Inc. and Brennan Newell, its CEO. As you read, you'll learn the four secrets of Diamond's success: Clarity, Commitment, Execution and Relationships. While these may sound like common-sense, Mom-and-apple-pie ideas, don't

think that you won't learn anything from reading this book. Through
a variety of real-life examples, Bud makes the ideas come alive.

Small-business owners, CEOs of public companies, middle
managers, leaders of not-for-profit organizations — anyone in a
position of leadership — will find numerous opportunities to put
the ideas and concepts presented in *Four Secrets of High Performing
Organizations* to work every day. At Walk the Talk Company, we use
many of the ideas suggested in this book every day.

When I saw the title of this book, I wondered if it would live up
to expectations. After reading it, I can unequivocally say that it does.
It is a quick read, full of insightful information on creating high
performing organizations. I invite you to follow Brennan Newell
and Diamond Inc.'s journey from mediocrity to high performance.
You'll enjoy the read but more importantly, you'll find this book to
be full of nuggets that you will be able to put to good use as you go
about creating your own high performing organization.

There is a fifth secret in *Four Secrets of High Performing
Organizations*. While the concepts of Clarity, Commitment,
Execution and Relationships are rather simple and straightforward,
it takes persistence, dedication and courage to apply them consistently.
Therein lies the challenge of the book. *Four Secrets of High Performing
Organizations* challenges the reader to go beyond his or her initial

thought, that "this is just common sense." It challenges us to be persistent, dedicated and courageous enough not just to espouse these four secrets, but to live them in our day-to-day lives. From personal experience, I can guarantee that those of you who take up the challenge and consistently apply these four secrets will create organizations whose performance will exceed your wildest dreams.

Eric Harvey is the co-author of *Walk the Talk* and *Get the Results You Want* and CEO of the Walk the Talk Company in Dallas, Texas.

· CONTENTS ·

SECTION 4
Execution

SECTION 5
Relationships

SECTION 6
The End...And a New Beginning

If there's one trend I've noticed in my work with corporate leaders during the last quarter century, it's the tendency to search for the silver bullet — the one program that will solve all of their problems. Top executives often add one management fad to another without giving adequate thought to the effect these combined initiatives have on the people in their organizations.

This is no surprise. In recent years, leaders have been invited to become Servant Leaders, Real Change Leaders, Transformational Leaders, Principle-Centered Leaders, Enlightened Leaders, Vanguard Leaders, Situational Leaders and Working Leaders. They have been exhorted to lead from the heart and to lead with soul. They've been told that leadership is an art and asked to take the leadership challenge.

By and large, their response has been to grab on to the latest fad, and institute one program after another. Here are just a few of the fads that leaders of U.S.-based companies have imposed on their people in the recent past: Reengineering, Balanced Scorecard, Economic Value Added, Total Quality Management, Six Sigma, Workout Sessions, and Do It Right the First Time. They've instituted team-building programs and written corporate mission, vision and values statements. They've reorganized into lean organizations, flat organizations, matrix organizations, and learning organizations. They've focused on changing their corporate culture and redoing their performance management programs. They've hired coaches and mentors. This list is far from being all-inclusive, but you get the picture.

Most of these programs begin with a lot of fanfare. There is a big kickoff meeting, in which senior leaders tout the benefits of the new program. This is followed by some training in which familiar concepts are given new names. Steering committees and implementation teams are created. Pilot projects are run. All of this takes a couple of years. And then senior leadership kicks off a new program. The net result is a wave of cynicism, expressed best by a phrase heard in all types of organizations — "flavor of the month."

It doesn't have to be this way. It's time to get back to the basics. I believe that there is a set of simple yet universal principles that, when applied rigorously and consistently, lead to organizational high performance. These principles are Clarity, Commitment, Execution and Relationships. By the time you finish this book, you will be able to categorize all of the fads mentioned above into one of these four principles.

I've written this book to provide leaders with a framework for creating their own high performing organizations. My intent is to provide a tool that will assist leaders in not getting blinded by the hype over the latest management fad. My advice to you is simple. Keep the four principles of Clarity, Commitment, Execution and Relationships in mind, and pay attention to what is already in place in your organization. If you do, you will be able to judiciously select and implement only those initiatives that will enhance the performance of your organization. You won't get caught in the flavor-of-the-month trap.

Reflections on Breadth and Simplicity

CHAPTER 1

A Simple Symbol
of a Far-Reaching Idea

"I'll be leaving now. Is there anything else you need before I go?"
Brennan Newell looked up from his e-mail to see his assistant
standing at the door.

"No thanks. I have a few more things to do, and then I'll be leaving
myself," he said.

"Don't forget you have that reporter coming to see you tomorrow."

"How could I? It's not every day that someone from a national
business magazine calls me up and tells me they want to do a profile
on me," he laughed.

"Well, you've really turned this place around in the time you've
been here," replied the assistant.

"Yes, but not without a lot of hard work from the people around
me — like you. Now get out of here and go home to your family.
Wear your best suit tomorrow. Maybe you'll get into a picture or two."

As his door closed, Brennan sat back and reflected on what he was going to say to the reporter. As he let his thoughts wander back over his 10 years as the CEO of Diamond Inc., he toyed with the one personal item on his desk. It was a cardboard bar coaster that Helen Yee, his Chief Operating Officer, had had laminated for him. She had given it to him the day she accepted his offer to join him at Diamond. On one side of the coaster was an advertisement for a local micro brew. On the other was a diagram in Brennan's handwriting. It looked like this.

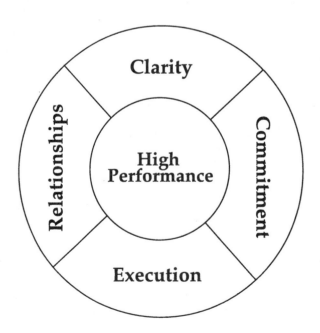

Introducing the Four Secrets

Brennan's mind drifted to 10 years before at a local café where he was meeting with Helen to ask her to become Diamond's COO. He had just been offered the Diamond CEO position. Helen was a top executive with Diamond's chief rival, Platinum, the biggest revenue producer and most profitable company in the industry. In fact, it was rumored that she might someday become the CEO there.

Brennan had met Helen Yee when he served with her on the board of an industry group. He admired her intelligence and pragmatic style. He knew that she was the kind of person he needed to help him turn around Diamond. Diamond was a company that had never lived up to its potential and Brennan knew it would be a tough sale, but he was convinced that, working together, he and Helen could create something special.

And they had. Diamond was now the undisputed industry

leader. Its market capitalization had quadrupled in the past 10 years. It had recorded 40 straight quarters of record growth and was one of Wall Street's darlings. Diamond had been included on several "Most Admired" lists for the past seven years, and had been recognized as "One of America's 100 Best Companies to Work For" for the past five years. When the company announced it was adding 100 positions to its sales force, it received more than 5,000 resumes. Brennan and Helen had turned a lumbering, slow-reacting company into a sleek profit-producing machine.

Brennan was on top of the world. Wall Street loved him. His board loved him. Diamond employees loved him. He was going to announce his retirement at the next board meeting and suggest that Helen be named his successor — something no one, not even Helen, knew yet. He had no doubt that the board would approve. Helen deserved just as much credit as he for Diamond's success.

As he looked at the coaster, he thought of his discussion with Helen that long-ago night. They had just finished their coffee when he made his pitch. He told her that he had big plans for Diamond and that he would need a partner to make those plans come true.

Helen was skeptical at first. "Brennan, you know I am the president of Platinum's biggest division and they like me there. With a little luck, I could end up in the top job some day."

"I know," said Brennan. "But I'm offering you the chance to become Diamond's COO right now. And I'm not going to be around forever. If things work out the way I think they will, Diamond will be first in the industry in the next decade, and you'll be the one running it."

"OK. You've got my interest," Helen said. "But what makes you think you can turn around Diamond, let alone overtake Platinum?"

"Breadth and simplicity," said Brennan.

"Go on," Helen said.

"That's it," he said.

"That's it?"

"Actually, yes," said Brennan. "All successful companies are built on a solid foundation. Breadth and simplicity are the foundation that will enable us to take Diamond to the top of our industry. Let me explain. First, you have to approach things from a broad perspective. The world is a complicated place. There is no silver bullet, no one path to success. To be successful, you must define a set of broad concepts that become the basis on which you build an organization. These concepts become the elements that drive your success."

"Makes sense," said Helen.

"But these elements of success need to be simple enough that everyone in the company can understand them and consistently apply them. It might sound paradoxical, but you need to be broad and simple at the same time," Brennan finished.

"Knowing you, I'm sure you already know what these broad but simple elements are," Helen said.

This was the opportunity for which Brennan had been waiting. He pulled out a felt-tipped marker, grabbed the coaster and started writing as he talked.

"I've been thinking about these ideas and refining them ever since I was in business school," he said. "I discussed them with the board in my interviews. I think it's why they hired me to run Diamond."

Brennan wrote "high performance" in the middle of the coaster, and drew a circle around it. Then he divided the space surrounding the circle into four quadrants. "Here's the way I see it," he said. "High performance, however you define it — profitability, stock price, P/E ratio, sales, whatever — is really dependent on four factors. If a company takes care of these four broad but simple factors, it has to succeed."

"You've got my attention," Helen said. "Don't keep me in suspense. What are these four magic factors?"

Brennan grinned. He had hoped this would interest Helen. She loved models and was always looking for simple ways to describe complex issues. In his mind, his four-factor model was elegant in its simplicity.

"OK. Factor Number One is Clarity. You've got to be clear about

who you are and where you're going. You have to make sure that
everyone in the company is clear about it too," he said.

Helen seemed interested, but wasn't sold yet.

Brennan took a deep breath and continued. "The second factor is
Commitment. You've got to make sure that everyone in the company
is committed to the company and where it's going. This is our job.
Well, right now it's still only my job, but it will be much easier if I
have you to help me," he said.

Helen seemed more interested now. She leaned forward and said,
"What are the other two factors?"

"Execution is the third," said Brennan. "No matter how good your
plans are, and how committed your people, you have to execute to be
successful. In my mind, execution means doing the right things, right.

"Finally, no business exists in a vacuum, so the last factor is
Relationships. We have to build solid, mutually beneficial relationships
with important outside groups. Our customers and suppliers come
to mind immediately. But I believe relationships go beyond those.
We live in a highly regulated world. We need to develop positive, not
adversarial, relationships with our regulators. We need to develop the
same types of relationships with the communities in which we do
business. We need to make all of these groups feel as if they are
our partners."

· SECTION 1: REFLECTIONS ·

Brennan was almost out of breath by the time he was finished. His face was flushed as he looked up at Helen and asked, "What do you think?"

CHAPTER 3

The Decision

Helen smiled. From her committee work with Brennan, she knew he was an intense guy. But she had never seen him this excited about anything.

"You've been working on these ideas for how long?"

"Ever since I was in business school," he said. "I've changed, added, deleted, gone back and added again. I think about this model all the time. I'm open to changing it, but this is what I'm going to start with when I take over at Diamond next month. Do you want to join me?"

Helen said, "This is a big decision for me. I have a lot of time invested in Platinum, and they've been good to me. Let me think about it."

With that, she picked up her purse. "I've got to get home," she said.

As she stood to leave, she put the coaster into her jacket pocket.

Brennan had another cup of coffee, paid the check and left.

Two days later, he received a courier delivery. Inside was the coaster, laminated. A handwritten note said, *"You've got me. You know I like to take complex issues and ideas and make them simple. Your ideas for running Diamond are just that. Give me a call to set up a time to discuss my responsibilities, compensation, start date, etc. HY"*

Now, 10 years later, Brennan sat back in his chair and smiled to himself. "And the rest, as they say, is history," he said aloud.

He turned off his laptop, packed his briefcase, called for the car and left for home. As usual, he was the last one to leave Diamond's offices. Tomorrow, he would be one of the first people there.

Beginning of a Dialogue

At precisely 10 o'clock the next morning, Brennan's assistant, clad in a new suit, knocked on the door and announced the arrival of journalist Patricia Henderson and photographer Matt Miloszewski. Brennan welcomed them. "I've invited Helen Yee to sit in on our chat," he said. "She's our COO and is as responsible for Diamond's success as anyone."

Patricia looked a little surprised but didn't say anything. Just then Helen came into the room and took a seat at the conference table with Brennan and Patricia. After coffee and the exchange of a few pleasantries, Patricia got down to business.

"Brennan, you've done a remarkable job making Diamond the Number One company in your industry. I'm sure our readers will be interested in hearing how you've done so much in such a short period of time."

"Thanks for your kind words, Patricia. But it hasn't been all my doing. Helen has played a big part in our success, as has everyone at Diamond," he said.

Helen smiled and said, "You are always one to share the credit and take the blame, Brennan. I agree that everyone at Diamond has made a big contribution to our success. But it all started with your ideas. I remember the night we sat at that café and you sketched out your ideas on that coaster. I knew then that Diamond was going to be a big success whether I joined or not. Your ideas were elegant in their breadth and simplicity."

Patricia was interested now. She recognized a good angle for a story when she saw one. "What are you talking about?"

"Brennan has always been a student of organizations. He brought his ideas about how effective organizations work to Diamond and put them to work here. You've seen the results," Helen said.

"Tell me more," said Patricia.

"On the night Brennan recruited me, he sketched out his ideas about high performance on the back of a coaster," Helen said. "I took that coaster with me and thought about what he said. When I decided to join Diamond, I had the coaster laminated and sent it to Brennan with a note accepting his offer. That's it right over there," she said, pointing to Brennan's desk.

CHAPTER 4

Patricia picked up the coaster. "Clarity, Commitment, Execution, Relationships," she said in a somewhat disappointed tone. "I thought I was going to be looking at the basis of Diamond's success. These ideas seem to be common sense and pretty simple."

"My point exactly," Brennan said. "People tend to over complicate things. Running a business isn't easy, but it's not as hard as a lot of people make it. Yes, these are basic ideas. But you'll notice that they encompass a lot. Breadth and simplicity are the foundation of this model. We've found that a broad perspective, coupled with simple ideas that are practiced every day, leads to great business results. We built Diamond on the foundation of Clarity, Commitment, Execution and Relationships. If you talk to anybody here, they can tell you about each of them, why they're important to our success, and how they get played out every day."

"You sound a bit evangelistic about this stuff," Patricia said. "I'm surprised. I expected you to be a hardheaded businessman."

"I am," said Brennan. "And these are the four things I'm the most hardheaded about. Right, Helen?"

"Right, Brennan," Helen said, as they both laughed.

"OK. If I've got this right, the two of you built Diamond into the powerful company it is today by applying four ideas: Clarity, Commitment, Execution, Relationships," Patricia said. "I'm hooked.

Tell me more."

Brennan looked at Patricia, "I'll explain it to you as best I can. But you really have to see it in practice to understand what I'm talking about. Let's take a walk. Bring your little recorder with you. I can get pretty excited about this stuff. You might not be able to keep up with your note taking as we walk and talk."

Patricia, who never went anywhere without her notepad, grabbed it and her recorder and followed Brennan.

Patricia's Notes

- High performance is the result of breadth and simplicity.

- A broad perspective must be coupled with simple ideas and concepts that are practiced every day.

- Four simple concepts are the secrets to high performance:
  - CLARITY of purpose and direction
  - The sincere COMMITMENT of everyone in the organization
  - Skillful EXECUTION of the things that matter
  - Mutually beneficial RELATIONSHIPS with important constituencies outside of the organization

Clarity

The Mission as Map

Brennan, Helen, Patricia and the photographer walked from his office to the reception area. It was nice, not ostentatious but well appointed.

"Look around. What do you see?" asked Brennan.

Patricia looked around. Several offices opened off a central area. In the open area, four administrative assistants were engaged in the typical activities: answering the phone, scheduling appointments, typing. There was a large conference room, which she suspected was the boardroom. "I'm not sure. This looks like any other large company's executive suite to me," she said.

"Look at the walls. What do you see?" Brennan asked.

Patricia looked. "I see some nice artwork, a lot of plaques given to Diamond for your philanthropic efforts, the Diamond mission — nothing out of the ordinary." She didn't say so, but she was getting a little annoyed. After all, she was the one who was supposed to be asking the questions.

Brennan said, "Take a look at the Diamond mission."

Patricia walked over to the framed mission statement and read it. Frankly, it didn't sound much different from what she had seen at other companies. She had often imagined that there was one mission writer who — for a fee, of course — produced mission statements for all of the companies in the country.

She said, "I don't mean any disrespect, but this mission doesn't seem all that different from mission statements I've seen at other companies."

"My point exactly," said Brennan. "All — or nearly all — companies have mission statements. It was a '90s thing to do. But in my experience, most missions have little more value than the paper on which they're printed.

"Our mission isn't all that unique. However, it is absolutely fundamental to Diamond's success."

Patricia seemed really confused now. "If your mission isn't unique, how can it be so critical to your success?" she asked.

Brennan smiled, "You tell her, Helen."

"Because we actually use it to run the business," Helen said.

Patricia waited for Helen to go on, but when it became apparent she wasn't going to continue, she asked, "Don't all companies do that?"

"No." Both Brennan and Helen spoke at once.

CHAPTER 5

"In fact, surprisingly few companies use their mission to actually guide their business. At Diamond, we use our mission to help us create a sense of clarity for everyone who works here," Brennan said. "Remember, I told you Clarity was one of our four success factors? Well, it all starts with our mission. Helen can tell you about how we came up with our mission."

"Let's go to my office," said Helen. "We can sit down there and I'll explain it to you."

The photographer, sensing he would not be needed for a while, asked for directions to the cafeteria and excused himself. Brennan turned to go to his office. "Aren't you coming?" Patricia asked.

"You're in good hands with Helen," he said.

Charting the Course

Once Helen and Patricia were settled in Helen's office, Helen began. "Brennan really does use the mission to run the Diamond business. I remember our first executive committee meeting. Brennan and I, the CFO, CIO, the VP of HR, the VP of strategic planning, our corporate counsel, and the presidents of our three operating divisions were there. You probably know this, but we have three operating divisions: Consumer Products, Private Label and Specialty Products. We're best known for our consumer products. Several Diamond brands have worldwide name recognition. Our Private Label and Specialty Products businesses are less well known but are powerhouses in their own right.

"Anyway, back to that first executive committee meeting. Brennan showed up with a bunch of large sticky notes. He said, 'We're here today to set the course for Diamond. Together, we're going to make this the Number One company in our industry.'

"There were a few smirks around the table. With the exception of Brennan and me, these were all Diamond old-timers. They had gotten used to the idea of being Number Two, and heading for being Number Three. You have to remember that in those days Diamond was not a bad company, just a mediocre one. Most people had become pretty complacent. They put in their time, collected their checks and hoped that their bonus this year would be bigger than last year. Bonuses always increased because our performance metrics were not a challenge. Anyone could meet them without breaking a sweat.

"Brennan handed out a set of sticky notes to everyone around the table. He asked them to think for a moment and write down the answer to this question: 'Why is Diamond in business?'

"It was interesting to watch. A few people started writing immediately. Most just sat there with stunned expressions on their faces. You'd have thought Brennan had asked them to explain uncertainty theory in 25 words or less.

"Brennan was patient. He waited 15 minutes until everyone had finished writing. Then he asked everybody to take their sticky note and post it on the white board at the front of the room. You could tell some people were uncomfortable with this, but Brennan was the boss so they figured they needed to play the game."

Helen took a sip of coffee and continued. "Looking back at it, the results were pretty much what you might expect. They were all over the place. At one extreme, there were a few stickies that said 'to make money.' At the other extreme, there was one that said, 'to offer products and services that will benefit mankind.' In between, there were stickies that said things like, 'to serve our customers well,' 'to provide high quality products,' 'to create shareholder value.' You get the idea.

"Brennan looked at the group and said, 'Look at this: 10 different people and 10 different answers to the simple question, 'Why are we in business?' If we don't know, how can we expect the 15,000 people in this company to know? We're not going to leave this question until we can all agree on one answer. I'm not sure what that answer is, but we'd better be able to come up with it if we're going to lead this company into the future.'

"So we spent the rest of that day discussing why we're in business. The answer to that question became our mission statement. We use it in our recruitment advertising. We use it in our job interviews. It's the first thing people hear in our orientation program. It is fundamental to us and provides clarity for every Diamond employee. We all know why we're here and what we are collectively trying to accomplish."

Patricia had been listening with rapt attention. "I hear what you're saying, but I'm a little confused. Your mission statement looks a lot like many other mission statements I've seen," she said. "What makes yours so special?"

"We use it to guide our business," said Brennan as he walked into the room and sat down. "We know our mission statement isn't unique. If you think about it, as you obviously have, Patricia, most corporate mission statements sound very similar — to be the best in our industry, to dominate our market, to be Number One, to provide exceptional shareholder returns, to create value. These are the things you'll find in the mission statements of most businesses.

"I believe we have been successful at Diamond because we've made our mission statement come alive for our people. To most Diamond people, our mission statement is more than the words on the plaque on the wall. They understand the markets we're in, who our customers are and what we need to do to serve them better than our competition. They know why we do the things we do, and how what they do every day fits into the big picture.

"Our mission is a leadership tool. We work very hard to help all of our people link it to their individual jobs. We go out of our way to help people make a connection between the Diamond mission and their jobs. We believe that if our people know and understand our mission, they will see that their jobs are important.

"Our leaders are responsible for helping their people see

exactly how their day-to-day responsibilities tie into our mission. They refer to the mission in performance feedback sessions. They reinforce their people who act in a manner that is consistent with the mission. They also redirect those few people who act in a manner that is inconsistent with our mission."

"And how do you get them to do all of that?" asked Patricia. "In most companies, you can hardly find someone who can repeat the mission without looking at a plaque or wallet card."

"The short answer is that everything proceeds from our mission," said Brennan. "I think this is a good time for you to meet Juan Ramirez, our VP of strategic planning. He can show you how we use our mission to establish clarity."

Mission Elements:
Strategic Guide

B rennan and Patricia left Helen and made their way to Juan Ramirez's office. After he introduced Patricia, Brennan said, "Juan, Patricia is interested in how we use our mission statement to drive our business. Would you take a few minutes to explain this to her?"

After Brennan left, Juan began. "What we do isn't complicated, really. The key is that we keep everything focused on our mission."

"How do you do that?" asked Patricia.

Juan sat back in his chair and said, "Our mission is at the heart of our strategic planning process. We create an annual business plan. Unlike a lot of companies, we actually use the plan to manage our business. When we begin the planning process every year, we start with the mission. Compatibility with our mission is the first hurdle for all strategic initiatives that are proposed. We don't consider any proposal unless everyone can agree that it is a good fit with our mission.

"This isn't as complicated as it sounds. We have a set of mission elements. These elements define what we need to do in order to fulfill our mission. If a proposal isn't directly related to one or more mission elements, it isn't a good strategic fit.

"What are these mission elements?" asked Patricia.

"We have three: product and service quality, customer satisfaction and financial performance," said Juan.

"We know that these mission elements are not right for every company. They're right for us. They provide the focus we need in order to plan what we are going to accomplish and then execute according to the plan."

"Sounds like common sense to me," said Patricia.

"That's the beauty of it," smiled Juan. "It is common sense, but in our case, it's applied common sense. When we review potential strategic initiatives, we review them in light of these mission elements. Those that are directly related to one or more of our elements get further consideration.

"Let me give you an example. Last year, our Consumer Division was considering a strategic initiative to reduce cycle time. Cycle time reduction gets a lot of play in the business press these days.

"But as you've probably already figured out, at Diamond we don't jump on the bandwagon of every management fad that comes around. When we choose to do something like this, we take it very seriously. We give it the resources and management support it needs to succeed.

"The first question the executive team asked the president of our Consumer Division was, 'What mission elements are related to cycle time reduction?' Her answer was 'customer satisfaction and financial performance. If we reduce cycle time we can avoid backorders and improve our inventory turns.'

"Once she got over that hurdle, she explained the cycle time reduction project her division was planning to implement. Her team had developed targets that would allow us to measure the project's success, and a plan that they believed would result in meeting or exceeding those targets. This part of their operating plan became part of the Diamond operating plan. We have similar conversations with each of our operating divisions every year.

"Let me tell you about how we write our strategies," Juan continued. "The format we use helps us lay the foundation for execution. All of our strategies follow the same format. They answer six questions. We use the answers to these questions to evaluate whether or not the proposed strategy is worth pursuing."

"What are these questions?" Patricia asked. Her notebook and pen in hand, she was prepared to write.

Juan listed the questions. "First, 'What is to be accomplished?' Second, 'Why is it important to accomplish it?' Third, 'How will it be accomplished?' Fourth, 'What resources are needed to accomplish it?' Fifth, 'What is the timeline for accomplishing it?' And sixth, 'Who is responsible for accomplishing it?'

"That's it?" asked Patricia. "The key to all of your strategies is those six simple questions? I was expecting something a lot more profound."

"Sorry to disappoint you," Juan said, "but these questions are not as simple as they may seem. To answer them well, you have to have a thorough grasp of the situation you are addressing and the ability to think through the details of how you are going to address it.

"We review and revise our strategies annually. When we are in particularly turbulent times, we review them every six months — just to make sure we're still headed in the right direction."

"I'm with you so far, but I still don't see how this is a competitive advantage for you," said Patricia.

"You're right," he said. "Most companies have a strategic plan. The difference here is that we distribute ours throughout the company. Our strategic plan is not a secret. We share it with all of our employees. We want them to know where we're going as a company. That way, it's easier for them to see how what they do every day fits into the big picture. Remember, our operating divisions use the strategic plan to develop their annual business plans. And individual employees use both the strategic and annual plans to develop their objectives.

"Distributing the strategic plan has the added advantage of helping us make sure that our annual business plans are driven by our strategic plan," Juan continued. "Our annual business plans set specific revenue and expense targets. To put it simply, each of our divisions figures out how much it plans to sell — in dollars and units — and what it is going to cost to sell it. To do this right, managers have to get all of the line functions — sales and marketing, procurement, production and distribution — involved. They bring in the accountants, IT and HR people as necessary.

"Once the divisional plans and the Diamond strategic plan are finalized, we communicate them to everyone in the organization. With the exception of very closely held information, the plans are posted on our intranet. Every Diamond employee knows the big-picture plan for every fiscal year.

"We move the strategic plan down through the company. Our three divisions use it to set their annual objectives. Individual employees use their division's plan to set their objectives. Every Diamond employee has annual objectives with performance metrics. Every person's objectives can be traced directly back to his or her division's annual plan.

"In fact, when we first started this approach, employee objectives had to be accompanied by a citation noting the page and paragraph of the division's annual plan to which they were related. We don't do this anymore because we found that it is unnecessary. Seeing how your individual work fits into the big picture has become such a part of Diamond's culture that we no longer need these citations. However, if you ask most people for a citation for one of their objectives, they can tell you."

"OK. I get it," said Patricia. "You establish clarity by using your mission to decide what gets into your annual business plan, and then you have everyone in Diamond develop objectives based on what's in the plan. That's all there is to clarity?"

"No," said Brennan, who seemed to have an uncanny ability for showing up at just the right time. "That's part of it, but not all. Our guiding principles play a big part in creating clarity, too."

"Guiding principles?" asked Patricia.

"Yes," said Brennan. "Come with me, and I'll take you to somebody who can explain."

"Thanks, Juan, I appreciate your time," Patricia said over her shoulder as she followed Brennan down the hall.

Guiding Principles
for Decision-Making

Brennan stopped three doors down the hall. "This is Sandra Nelson. She's our VP of HR. She is probably the best person to talk to regarding the Diamond guiding principles. Sandra, this is Patricia. She's doing an article on Diamond and wants to know about the our guiding principles."

"Hi, Patricia. It's nice to meet you. Why don't we sit over here? Would you like something to drink? Coffee? Water?"

"Water would be great," Patricia said.

Sandra's assistant brought two bottles of water. "What would you like to know about the Diamond guiding principles?" she asked.

"First of all, what are they? What do you mean by the term guiding principles?" Patricia asked.

"Think of it this way," said Sandra. "Most people have a set of values they use to guide their lives. We've taken that concept and extended it to our organization."

"Tell me more," Patricia said.

"Let me ask you a question, Patricia. What are the few principles or beliefs that are most important to you personally?"

Patricia thought for a minute. "My family, personal honesty... I don't know...."

"That's OK," said Sandra. "Bear with me for a minute."

Patricia nodded.

She continued, "You say your family is one of the most important things to you. Do you ever consider your family when you have to make a decision?"

"All the time," Patricia said.

"Can you give me a specific example?" Sandra asked.

Patricia thought for a moment. "Last year I was offered an opportunity to head up our editorial offices in Chicago. It was a great offer. But I turned it down because my kids had just started at a new school that they really liked, and I didn't want them to have to move."

"So your concern for your family guided your decision-making process in this case," said Sandra.

"Yes."

"That's exactly how guiding principles work. We have four Diamond guiding principles. We explain them to everyone the first day they start work. Then we tell them, 'Whenever you're in doubt, think about the guiding principles. They'll help you make a good decision.'

"You used your personal guiding principle of family to help you make what was probably a very difficult personal decision. We ask Diamond people to use the Diamond guiding principles to help them make business decisions. Our business environment is full of change and ambiguity. The Diamond guiding principles help our people make good decisions when there is no clear-cut answer."

"What are these guiding principles? How did you develop them?" Patricia asked.

"As I've said, there are four Diamond guiding principles: Respect for the Individual, Integrity, Nimbleness, Service. We didn't develop them. We discovered them."

"Discovered them? What did you do, mount a search party?" Patricia laughed.

Sandra smiled. "You could say that. Diamond is an old and proud company. Granted, we had been living on our reputation before Brennan got here. But he was smart enough to know that we had a proud tradition — a tradition of being fair to our people, playing by the rules, being quick to respond to opportunities and standing by our products and services.

"You've probably already heard about our 'Why are we in business?' meeting when Brennan first got here."

Patricia nodded and Sandra went on. "About a month after that meeting, Brennan got us all together again. This time when he handed out the stickies, he asked us to list the reasons — one per sticky — we were proud to be a part of Diamond.

"After everybody posted their stickies, we looked at what was there. We started looking for themes — grouping those that seemed to fit together and leaving the outliers alone. We finally agreed there were four common threads that ran through everything.

"We focused on those and gave each of them a name. The results were 'Respect for the Individual, Integrity, Nimbleness and Service.' We took the individual stickies that formed these groupings and used them to write three- or four-sentence descriptors of what we meant by each heading.

"When we were finished," Sandra continued, "we felt we had captured the good things about Diamond's culture — things that it makes sense to reinforce with all our people. These became our guiding principles. We're proud of them. They capture the spirit of Diamond. Our shorthand name for them is the 'Diamond Way.' We ask our people to keep the Diamond Way in mind as they go about their day-to-day business. We use the terms guiding principles, values and Diamond Way interchangeably. Whatever we call them, all of our senior leaders use them to guide their actions. With the leaders setting the example, we believe we have the right to ask all Diamond people to use them to guide their actions and decisions as well."

"You mean everybody's behavior is consistent with these guiding principles all the time?" Patricia asked.

"No," said Sandra. "These guiding principles set some pretty high standards. We all try to live up to them. Sometimes we slip. Sometimes we even have trouble deciding which behaviors are consistent with them and which are not. But what makes Diamond different from a lot of places is that we use our slips as learning opportunities. We keep trying and we keep getting better at it.

"We don't have a big policy and procedure manual. In fact, if it weren't for regulatory requirements, I doubt we would have policies and procedures at all. Our procedure manual is minimal because we explain the guiding principles to our people and ask them to use them as a guide for their personal behavior and decision-making at work.

"This is interesting," said Patricia. "I think I'm starting to get a pretty good idea of how you manage clarity around here."

"Think about it for a while. I think you'll see that it makes sense," Sandra said. "Like most things we do at Diamond, it's a deceptively simple concept. We work hard at making it work."

Sandra stood up. "It's getting late, and I have a few things to do before I leave for the day. Let me get you back to Brennan. I'm sure you have a few more questions for him."

Getting Clear on Clarity

"Well, how did it go?" Brennan asked Patricia.

"It was interesting," Patricia said. "I'm starting to get a pretty good grasp on Clarity, but I haven't heard anything about Commitment, Execution or Relationships."

"Tell me what you learned about Clarity, Diamond style," said Brennan.

"Well, as best I can tell, it revolves around two things: the Diamond mission and the Diamond guiding principles," said Patricia.

"Go on," said Brennan.

"The mission is a statement of why you are in business. It helps you make strategic decisions. It also drives your business planning process at the corporate and division levels," she continued.

"What else?"

"Oh, I almost forgot. Diamond employees use the business plans as a guide when they are setting annual objectives," Patricia said.

"Right," said Brennan. "Now what about the Diamond Way?"

"The guiding principles, you mean. You use them as guides for day-to-day decision-making," she said. "They're kind of like the personal values we all use to guide our life decisions."

"You've been talking with Sandra," Brennan laughed. "She's the one who came up with that analogy, and it's a good one. In fact, I've come to think of our guiding principles as the Diamond values. They are core to us as an organization. We work hard to make sure we act in a manner consistent with them.

"I expect everyone in Diamond to embrace our guiding principles. I'm toughest on myself and the people closest to me when it comes to them. If we don't exemplify them, how can we expect the other 14,900 Diamond people to?"

"It seems so simple," said Patricia. "If I get it, the Diamond principle of Clarity goes something like this. One, decide why you're in business. Two, communicate this to everybody. Three, build your corporate and operating unit business plans around it. Four, have people base their objectives on their business unit business plans."

"And five, give everybody feedback on how they're doing," said Brennan.

CHAPTER 9

"But that's only half of it," said Patricia, warming to the task. "The second part is to identify the things that are core to your company and publish them. You call them guiding principles, but you could just as easily call them values. They define the Diamond Way. You expect everyone — especially leaders — to act in a manner consistent with these guiding principles."

"What else?" Brennan asked.

Patricia thought for a few seconds. "You tell people to use the guiding principles as guides for decision-making, and you trust them to make the right decisions."

Brennan sat back in his chair and smiled. "You've got it."

"But it seems so simple," Patricia said.

"That's it exactly," Brennan replied. "I never claimed that this stuff is rocket science. It's not even brain surgery," he laughed. "But seriously, that's a mainstay of my leadership credo — simplicity. Breadth is the other part. And don't forget, we haven't discussed Commitment, Execution or Relationships yet."

"I know," said Patricia.

"Well, why don't you come back tomorrow and we'll talk a little more about the other three simple ideas that make up the Diamond leadership philosophy," Brennan said.

"It's a deal. I'll be here at nine."

Patricia's Notes

CLARITY

- Mission is the first key to Clarity. High performing organizations use their Mission to drive their business.

- Mission Elements define what it takes to achieve the Mission and to help the Mission come alive for people in the organization.

- An organization's Mission should drive its Strategic Business Plan.

- Individual Performance Objectives should be developed using the Strategic Business Plan as a base.

- An organization's Values or Guiding Principles help members know how to act in ambiguous situations. They must reflect the very fabric of the organization and everybody must practice them.

- Formal leaders must be role models for the organization's Values or Guiding Principles. Leaders must conduct themselves in a manner consistent with the Guiding Principles at all times.

Commitment

Finding "Diamonds in the Rough"

Patricia arrived at Brennan's office at 8:45 a.m. the next day. Brennan looked up as his assistant ushered her in.

"You're early."

"I hope that's not a problem," she said. "I was thinking about some of the things I heard here yesterday. I was up, so I decided to come early and get a good start on the day."

Brennan smiled. "No problem at all. In fact, it's one of the things I wanted to discuss with you today. Arriving early because you're interested in and excited about what you're doing is one of the qualities of a 'Diamond in the Rough.'"

"Diamond in the Rough?" Patricia asked.

"That's what we call people who are good candidates for employment here," Brennan chuckled. "Remember yesterday, I said that Commitment is one of the four factors on which Diamond is built?"

Patricia nodded.

"Our selection process is where we begin building commitment," Brennan said. "We refer to promising candidates as 'Diamonds in the Rough.' All Diamonds in the Rough share certain qualities. An eagerness to get on with things is one of those qualities.

"I won't bore you with a description of all of the Diamond in the Rough characteristics. But you should know that we use them in our selection process. We believe that if we find people who are a good fit for us — Diamonds in the Rough — it's easier to build commitment."

"But don't you worry about getting too inbred?" Patricia asked. "If everybody is the same, where will you get new ideas? Who will challenge the status quo?"

Brennan smiled. "Another Diamond in the Rough characteristic — diversity of thinking, the ability and willingness to challenge accepted practices. Are you looking for a job? You seem as if you would fit in real well around here.

"You're right about valuing diversity of thinking, though. We aren't looking for people who are all the same. In fact, one of the things we prize most is diversity of thought. If you read our 'Respect for the Individual' guiding principle, you'll see that we really prize and encourage differences of opinion. That's the way we learn from each other.

CHAPTER 10

"No, Diamonds in the Rough aren't automatons. They're unique, independent individuals who we think will mesh well with the unique and independent individuals who are already here.

"Let me get back to our selection process. It begins with a paper review of an individual's credentials. If he or she seems to have the skill set we're looking for, we'll bring him or her in for an interview.

"The first interview focuses almost exclusively on Diamond in the Rough characteristics. Several Diamond people participate: HR, the hiring manager, potential co-workers, colleagues from other departments.

"On that day, we spend a lot of time selling Diamond."

"But this is a preliminary interview," said Patricia. "Why do you sell your company to somebody you might not want?"

Brennan smiled. "Because we want everyone who interacts with Diamond to have a positive experience. Interviewing for a job is stressful. We want to minimize people's stress and help them sell themselves to us. We also want them to leave feeling good about us.

"You'd be surprised. We have a lot of people working here who were referred by people we had interviewed but not invited back. To me, that's a good measure of how well we're doing at creating positive experiences for our candidates.

"If people get by that initial, rather grueling — for us and them —

screening, we invite them back to meet again with the hiring manager. He or she focuses this interview on the technical part of the job, overall chemistry with his or her department and, of course, the Diamond in the Rough characteristics.

"While a lot of people are involved in our selection process, the hiring manager always makes the final decision. After all, he or she has to live with the person.

"We feel that if we start with people who are a good fit, we are a long way toward gaining their commitment. One of the biggest mistakes of my career was hiring an individual with excellent technical skills, experience and references, but who just didn't 'feel' quite right to me. He was gone in nine months, but those nine months were hell — for him and for me.

"So we spend a lot of time finding the people who are likely to flourish here. It often takes a little time on the front end, but it saves a lot of headache, heartache and money in the end."

"I get the picture," said Patricia. "It's not easy to get a job at Diamond."

"You're right, it's not," said Brennan. "But we very seldom make an offer that is not accepted. By the time we're ready to make an offer, candidates are ready to join us."

· CHAPTER 11 ·

Building Commitment
from Day One

B rennan said, "Let's talk about some of the other ways we go
about building commitment."

Patricia nodded and started her recorder. "I'm all ears."

Brennan took a deep breath and plunged in. "The job of building
commitment gets underway in earnest the first day on the job.
Since we start people in their new jobs on Monday, we have
orientation sessions every Monday. A member of the Diamond
Executive Committee or I kick off every orientation session done at
headquarters. We do these orientation sessions whether one person
or 100 are joining us on a given Monday.

"People who join us at remote locations like sales offices or
manufacturing and R&D facilities see a tape of me welcoming
them to Diamond. It's essentially what I say to the people I meet
in person — only a little more polished, since I had a script and

did numerous takes," he chuckled.

"What else happens in this orientation?" Patricia asked.

"A lot of the kinds of things that you'd expect. We explain our benefits and get people enrolled in a health program and the 401k. We do a brief review of Diamond's history. Most of the people who join us know about our recent history, so we provide them with a quick look at the 120 years that preceded the past 10.

"Also, we do some things that you might not expect. We discuss the Diamond guiding principles in detail. We have a brief video that describes each of them. Then we do some workshops, case studies really, to get people thinking about various situations they might face. We help them reason out what they might do, using the guiding principles to make decisions.

"The goal of all this is to make people feel welcome and included. We spend so much time on our orientation because we want to make sure that people who join us feel as if we treat them with the respect and dignity they deserve. We want all Diamond people to feel that they are valued for their unique backgrounds, talents and skills."

"Who conducts these orientation sessions?" Patricia asked. "Human Resources?"

"Yes and no. HR handles the technical stuff, like benefits sign-up.

But we select a new group of orientation leaders annually. It's really a quarter-time position. They keep their regular jobs, with a somewhat reduced workload. They conduct the sessions every week and have some time to prepare and debrief each week. Conducting the orientation sessions becomes part of their annual objectives. We usually find that our best people are the ones who apply for the orientation positions."

"Don't people see this as potentially damaging to their careers? I mean one-fourth of their objectives are taken up by non-value-added work," Patricia said.

"On the contrary, leading orientation sessions is one of the most important things a Diamond person can do," said Brennan. "Orientation is a critical component of the commitment building process, and Commitment..."

"...is one of your four success factors," Patricia laughed.

"Now you're getting it," said Brennan.

Patricia smiled. "I'm beginning to see how Diamond took simple concepts and used them to create a business powerhouse," she thought.

Building Commitment Through Learning

"I see how your orientation differs from that of a lot of companies," said Patricia. "On the day I started with my company, they gave me a bunch of benefit forms to fill out and return, introduced me to the guy in the office next to mine, showed me where the bathroom was and told me how to get to the cafeteria. That was my orientation."

"Unfortunately, that's the way it is at a lot of places," said Brennan. It was like that here too, until we changed things."

"Selection and orientation. What else do you do to build commitment?" asked Patricia.

"Let's take another walk," said Brennan.

This time they left the building in which Brennan had his office, and walked across the street. "Welcome to our Learning Center," said Brennan. "Learning is one of the ways in which we build commitment.

• SECTION 3: COMMITMENT •

This is where we teach our people the Diamond Way.

"The truth be told, the technical information we present in our training is not much different from what you will find at most successful companies. The difference here, or at least we believe it's a difference, is that we focus on applying the concepts we teach. We teach our people how to use what they learn in a manner consistent with the Diamond mission and guiding principles."

By this time, they were inside the lobby of the Learning Center. "We conduct almost all of our in-house training right here. Let's take a look at what's going on today."

They walked over to a kiosk and Brennan tapped the interactive screen to get the schedule for the day.

"It seems as if we're doing a lot of sales training today. We have a class of brand new reps in one room, an advanced class in another and a sales manager class in a third. We also are conducting a 'Presenting with Impact' class and orientation leader training."

"What's going on over there?" asked Patricia.

"That's our self-paced instruction center," answered Brennan. "We've found that certain training does not have to be delivered in a classroom setting — things like time and stress management, software skills, anything that is more information- than relationship-oriented. Our people reserve time in the Center and then learn at their own pace."

"On company time?" asked Patricia.

"Of course," said Brennan. "The company benefits, so why shouldn't we provide people the time to learn? We do find that some people like to come in before or after work, so the Center is open from 5:30 a.m. to 11:00 p.m. We have a 90 percent usage rate on the equipment.

"We also deliver our self-paced instruction via the Web. We put the courses up on the Diamond intranet. That way, people don't have to come to the Learning Center. They can access the material at their desk or at home. We've been getting a lot of positive feedback on our Web-based instruction.

"How much training do your people get in a year?" Patricia asked.

"It depends. But we budget 80 hours per year per person — not counting self-paced instruction. People work out the time they spend in training with their manager," said Brennan. "In any given year, some people may be below 80 hours, and others may exceed it."

"Eighty hours — that's two weeks," said Patricia.

"Yes, it seems like a lot," Brennan said. "But you have to remember that we are in a highly competitive environment. Market demands and technology change rapidly. Our competition is always looking for a chink in our armor. We want to make sure that our people have the knowledge and skills necessary to ensure Diamond's success. We think of it as an investment, not an expense.

"Another thing, we conduct most of our training ourselves. There are a lot of fine training vendors out there and we purchase materials from quite a few of them. However, we see training as a culture-building activity. As I've said, we use this Learning Center to help our people develop the skills they need to keep us competitive, but we also use it to teach them the Diamond Way. Every program makes an explicit connection to one or more of our mission elements and guiding principles.

"We like to use Diamond people to conduct our training. In fact, an assignment to the Learning Center is quite a plum. We use these assignments to develop our high potential people. We've found that people really learn a subject when they have to teach it. After two years here, most people are ready to take on a job with significant responsibility.

"Of course, we have a small group of education professionals who spend their careers at the Learning Center. Teaching and learning is their career path. However, over the years, several of these people have decided to try their hand at an operational job. Most of them have done quite well, too."

"You develop people by having them develop others?" asked Patricia.

· CHAPTER 12 ·

"In a word, yes," said Brennan. "Why don't you wander around
here for a while? Feel free to drop in on any of the classes. But
don't be surprised if the instructor asks you to introduce yourself to
the group. That's one of the ground rules at the Learning Center —
anyone who drops in on a class must introduce herself and say what
she's doing there. You can tell them you're writing an article about
Diamond, and I invited you spend time here seeing how we
develop people.

"If you spot an open carrel, feel free to log on and check out
some of our online courses. You can use my password," said
Brennan. He wrote it on the back of a business card.

After Brennan left, Patricia visited a sales class, where she was
asked to play the part of a disgruntled customer in a role-play.
Next, she observed Diamond people making presentations and
critiquing one another in the "Presenting with Impact" class. She
was impressed with how willing people seemed to give and receive
feedback. One of the instructors told her that peer feedback is a
cornerstone of all Diamond Learning Center programs.

"Trust and openness are keys to our success. We expect
Diamond people to help each other learn and grow — not just
here, but on the job as well," she said. "We work hard to create an
open, trusting atmosphere where people can learn from each other."

From what she observed, Patricia thought they succeeded quite well.

She spotted an open carrel and logged on to a one-hour self-paced course on stress management. After she was finished, she promised herself she would resume the daily exercise regimen she had let lapse during the past few months.

By this time, it was close to 6:00 p.m. As she left the Learning Center, she saw the light was on in Brennan's office. She thought about dropping in to chat about what she had seen at the Learning Center, but decided to go home and review her notes for the article. She had an 11:00 a.m. appointment with Brennan the next day to discuss the Diamond Reward System.

Rewarding Commitment

"So you're here to talk about our approach to rewards,"
Brennan said, as he ushered Patricia into his office and offered her
a cup of coffee.

"Yes."

"Rewards are another tool we use to build commitment,"
Brennan began. "The concept behind our rewards system is simple.
We believe that people continue to do the things for which they are
rewarded. Therefore, we focus on rewarding people for performance
that enhances our bottom line and reflects the Diamond Way.

"This is not as difficult as it might seem at first glance. If people
meet their objectives, they get rewarded. If they exceed their objectives, their rewards exceed the rewards of the people who merely
meet their objectives.

"Diamond people get two types of monetary rewards—salary

increases and stock options. Like most companies, we use salary surveys to set our annual salary increases. We attempt to position ourselves in the upper quartile of companies in our industry and in the communities in which we operate. We want to attract the top talent, so we pay very competitive salaries. We don't position ourselves as the top-paying company in our industry. We believe we can attract the talent we need by being in the top quartile.

"We also have a very liberal stock option program," Brennan continued. "We encourage employee ownership of Diamond stock. We've found that options are the best tool to get our people invested in our company. All of our employees participate in the stock option program.

"Employees receive options based on their performance. These options are not automatic. Each manager has a certain allotment of options available. The manager may choose to grant them all to one individual or to split them evenly among all of his or her employees. This rarely happens though, as our managers are pretty good at differentiating employee performance.

"Our compensation department is available to advise managers having a difficult time assigning options. We want options to be an incentive—not a disincentive — for our people, so we work hard at ensuring the best performers get the best option packages," said Brennan.

"So the people who get the most options are the people who did the best in their performance against objectives?" Patricia asked.

"Yes and no," said Brennan. "Intangibles are often the deciding factor in allocating options. We focus on results, but we are also interested in how those results were achieved. For example, people who consistently set a positive model for the Diamond Way are likely to receive a better option grant than those who merely conduct themselves in accordance with our guiding principles."

"I think I know the answer to this question," Patricia said, "but I'll ask it anyway. What happens to people whose behavior does not reflect your guiding principles?"

"The first year that happens they get no options," Brennan said. "There usually isn't a second year. People either get the message and change their behavior, or we ask them to leave us. We're not very tolerant of people who aren't willing to conduct themselves in a manner consistent with our guiding principles.

"You know Patricia, with all of this talk about salary and options, I'm falling into the trap I always tell our people to avoid," Brennan said. "From what I've said so far, you might think I believe compensation and benefits are the key to an effective reward system. You do have to pay people well or you run the risk of losing them to your competition. But compensation and benefits are not the key to an effective reward system. Leadership is. We rely on our managers to reinforce the Diamond Way, and there's no doubt that compensation and stock options are two of the biggest tools they have at their disposal.

"However, I believe that meaningful conversations between people and their managers are more important than financial rewards. People are interested in what their boss thinks about them and their performance. They want a pat on the back when they do something good. And believe it or not, they also want to hear about it when they make a mistake or cause a problem."

Brennan continued, "Our managers know that two of their most important jobs are reinforcing high performance and appropriate behavior, and redirecting low performance and inappropriate behavior. This goes back to what I said as we began this conversation. 'People continue to do the things for which they get rewarded.' The reverse is also true. Most people make a change in behaviors that earn them negative feedback from their boss.

"We tell our managers to make sure that all of the people who work for them know what they are supposed to do, and have the tools they need to be able to do a good job.

"We use development opportunities as a reward, too. Diamond managers go out of their way to find assignments that will help their people grow and prepare for future promotions. We stretch our best people because we know that really good people find new challenges rewarding."

Mutual Accountability

"We also reward people who are willing to sacrifice for the good of the entire business," Brennan said.

"This all sounds very good in theory," Patricia said, obviously skeptical, "but how does it work in practice?"

"Let me give you an example," said Brennan. "Mutual accountability is one of the things we strive for around here. Mutual accountability is just a fancy way of saying, 'We're all in this together.' We want our people to do two things when it comes to mutual accountability. First, we want them to keep an eye on the big picture. Never forget that we're in business to serve our customers. Second, we want them to help each other out. We tell them, 'Focus on doing your job well, but be willing to lend a hand to a co-worker or department that needs your help.'"

Patricia nodded but still looked somewhat confused.

Brennan leaned toward her and said, "OK. Let's be even more specific. In simple terms, sales and marketing people have the responsibility for creating a demand for Diamond products. Right?" Patricia nodded.

"On the other hand, manufacturing people have the responsibility for producing high quality Diamond products at a low cost," he continued.

"I'm with you so far," Patricia said.

"One of the ways that sales and marketing can create demand for Diamond products is by offering a variety of SKUs. This is especially true in our Consumer Division. Some people prefer our products in individual packs, others like three-packs, still others like six-packs. So if you're a sales and marketing person, you want the ability to present our products in a variety of packaging presentations. In this way, you're likely to have a package that meets the needs of more customers than if you have only one presentation. To put it simply, more packaging presentations are likely to equal more sales, and more sales add up to more rewards for the sales and marketing people. Makes perfect sense, doesn't it?" Brennan asked.

Patricia nodded.

He smiled and continued, "Now let's think about the manufacturing people. They don't generate sales or any other type of revenue. In fact, one could argue that not only do they not bring in any money; they spend a lot of it. It costs a lot to operate a plant. Our manufacturing people are good. They know that they can contribute to our bottom line by decreasing their costs. They operate by the old saying, 'A penny saved is a penny earned.'"

"I'm still with you," said Patricia.

"Good," Brennan said. "One of the ways you can keep costs down in a manufacturing environment is to set up the equipment, lock it in and do long production runs. A lot of time and money are spent on equipment changeover."

"And the more SKUs you have, the more often you need to change over your equipment," said Patricia.

Brennan smiled. "Exactly."

"Now let's look at how this can impact our reward system," he continued. "Sales and marketing people get rewarded for selling a lot of product. One of the best ways for them to sell a lot of product is to provide customers with a wide variety of choices.

"On the other hand, manufacturing people get rewarded for keeping their costs down. One of the best ways of keeping your manufacturing costs down is to have fewer presentations, which will allow you to have longer production runs, which will increase your efficiencies, which means lower costs — and higher rewards for the manufacturing people."

"I can see where this can cause some problems," said Patricia. "People are at cross-purposes."

"They don't have to be," said Brennan. "As I said, we focus on mutual accountability. We try to create win-win situations wherever we can. We handled the sales and marketing/manufacturing problem by getting our manufacturing people involved very early in the new product development process. Manufacturing participates in all of our discussions regarding package design.

"Before we did this, we would sometimes find ourselves in a situation in which sales and marketing had committed to a particular package design only to find out that our manufacturing facilities didn't even have the equipment necessary to produce that type of package. Not only would this delay product launches — which had a negative impact on sales and marketing people's rewards, but manufacturing costs also would skyrocket as they had to buy and install new equipment, hurting their chances for excellent rewards. Nobody would be happy and everyone would be pointing their finger at the other guy," Brennan said.

"Several years ago we restructured our reward system to focus on overall profitability. We focus first on divisional performance and then Diamond's corporate performance. Individual performance against goals is a distant third. Now, we find that individuals and groups who previously were at odds with one another work well together.

"To get back to the example we've been using, our Consumer Division manufacturing people understand the need for a variety of product presentations, and accept the fact that somewhat frequent changeovers are an integral part of our business. They've gotten quite good at streamlining the changeover process and increasing the equipment up time.

"On the other hand, their sales and marketing counterparts have gotten much more sophisticated in understanding our customers' needs and wants. This makes them less likely to initiate a packaging change every time a customer says, 'It would be great if....' They also have gained an appreciation for what it takes for their manufacturing colleagues to make what appears at first glance to be a simple change."

"It makes sense to me," Patricia said. "But it seems almost too simple."

Brennan sat back in his chair. "You might think of this as common sense, or a typical cross-functional continuous improvement project — which it is. However, it would not work if we did not get our act together and put the rewards systems into place to facilitate it. Remember, people continue to do the things for which they get rewarded. By creating a reward system that fosters and encourages collaboration and mutual accountability, we are solving several problems. Interdepartmental bickering has gone down. Sales continue to rise and manufacturing costs continue to improve."

Leading for
Commitment, Part 1

B rennan and Patricia were having lunch in the Diamond cafeteria two days later. Patricia took a bite of her salad. "I'm starting to get a feel for how you build commitment around here: selection, orientation, education, reward systems. They all make sense individually, but when you put them together as you have, they reinforce one another."

"Thanks," said Brennan. "But we haven't talked about the most important aspect of the Commitment factor yet."

Patricia looked a bit surprised, but waited. By now, she knew Brennan was leading up to something.

"Leadership," he said. "Everyone here has the responsibility to build commitment by exercising leadership. We expect all of our people to do whatever it takes to build commitment and create a collective sense of spirit. People can be leaders no matter what their job," Brennan said.

"When I visit with customers, they tell me they can always spot a Diamond sales rep. They say that our people drive cleaner cars, dress better and are more prepared. To me this is leadership. When young people join our sales organization, they listen to what we say in training but more importantly, they see what their more experienced colleagues actually do in the field. And what they see is a group of professionals who care about the image they create for Diamond. They see a whole sales force of leaders who don't even have to say anything to lead. Their actions speak for themselves."

Brennan continued, "It's the same in our manufacturing and distribution locations. Diamond people look out for one another. When one of our people sees a colleague engaging in a potentially unsafe act, the first person leads by stopping whatever he or she is doing and bringing the potential consequences of the unsafe act to the other person's attention. They do this because they care about their co-workers and because it is the responsible thing to do for the business.

"You'll find a million tiny examples of people stepping up and leading every day. One of the things you'll notice around here is how punctual people are. We start and end meetings on time. If the person who is conducting the meeting doesn't take it upon himself or herself to manage time appropriately, you can bet someone else will.

"People also show leadership through little courtesies. When meetings end, the people who are in attendance put their coffee cups and napkins in the trash. They do this because they realize other Diamond people are likely to be in that conference room in a few minutes, and they shouldn't have to pick up other people's trash as they begin their meeting. If someone forgets, you can be sure that one of his colleagues will remind him — either by actions or words.

"We encourage people to lead by their actions, and we reward them for it. Managers are always on the lookout for someone who has stepped up and led. When they find leadership in action, they make a point of telling the person about it. I could go on and on about this because I'm proud of our people and the way they accept the responsibility of leadership."

"What about the people in formal leadership roles?" Patricia asked. "With the high expectations you have of non-management people, you must have really high expectations of your managers."

"We do," said Brennan. "We tell our managers that in addition to meeting their business goals, they have the important responsibility of building and sustaining the Diamond culture and creating the next generation of Diamond leaders. We're serious about this. We hold them accountable for it.

"We insist that our leaders treat everyone fairly and with

respect. We never let them forget that they are the link between Diamond and our people. Therefore, we expect them to communicate with their people, making sure that they are well informed. We also tell them that communication works two ways. We want our leaders to encourage their people to express their opinions and ideas. And, when someone has a good idea, we want our leaders to act on it. Diamond leaders are open to good ideas and suggestions, no matter what the source." Brennan paused to let what he'd just said sink in.

"We tell our leaders to make sure that their people know what's expected of them, have the tools and resources they need to do their job, and then get out of the way and let them perform. We want our people to learn and grow. Our leaders encourage their people's development. They recognize them for doing a good job, and they help them improve in areas where they are a little weak.

"Like I just said, leadership at Diamond is as much about building the culture and developing people as it is about meeting business goals."

"If I know you — and I think I'm beginning to — you have some pretty clear ideas of what it takes to be a Diamond leader," Patricia said.

"Right again," said Brennan. "Diamond leaders share two important characteristics. First, they all are highly effective as people and second, they have well-developed leadership skills. We believe that personal effectiveness is a prerequisite for leadership effectiveness."

"Whoa there, those are some pretty broad concepts you're tossing around," said Patricia. "Personal effectiveness? Leadership effectiveness? What do you do — have all of your leaders read *The Seven Habits of Highly Effective People?*"

Brennan chuckled. "That might not be a bad idea. I like what Stephen Covey has to say. But that's not the point. I believe people must be responsible adults, able to function at a high level of personal effectiveness, before they can even think about leading others."

"What's the magic formula?" Patricia asked.

"There is no magic formula, but there are several characteristics we look for in aspiring leaders. First of all, we look for people who demonstrate strong personal integrity. If our leaders don't conduct themselves in a responsible and ethical manner, we can't expect our people to do so.

"Second, we want leaders who have a strong sense of personal responsibility. We are interested in developing people who have demonstrated the willingness to identify problems and solve them on their own.

"Third, we look for people who are aware of themselves and those around them. We believe that in order to be an effective leader, you must first have an understanding of who you are — your strengths and weaknesses. You must also have the ability to understand the people around you. You could call this characteristic empathy.

"Next we look for people who are adaptable. We have found that good leaders are more flexible than they are rigid.

"We also insist on strong communication skills. Our leaders must be comfortable in front of a group as well as in one-to-one conversation. They also need to have the ability to express themselves well in writing.

"Finally, we look for people who are appropriately ambitious. By that I mean people who want to build a career with us by stepping up and leading. We're not interested in people who are trying to 'claw their way to the top.' But we have found that personal ambition, applied appropriately, is a common characteristic of successful Diamond leaders.

"These things work for us. We don't pretend to suggest that they're right for other companies, but they define the type of person we want as a leader around here. I believe that every business has to set basic standards of personal effectiveness that are prerequisites for leadership. Without a level of personal effectiveness, no one can successfully lead others," said Brennan.

"Let me make sure I've got them," said Patricia. "You look for

· CHAPTER 15 ·

these things when identifying potential future leaders at Diamond: personal integrity, the willingness to take responsibility, self-awareness and empathy, adaptability, strong communication skills and ambition."

"Yes," said Brennan. "That covers it."

Leading for
Commitment, Part 2

B y now, they were finished with their lunch and on their way
back to Brennan's office.

"Once we have identified potential leaders, we focus on
developing them in three areas," Brennan said.

"What are they?" asked Patricia.

"First, they need to have the ability to develop and communicate
a clear and compelling vision of the future they are creating. Second,
we expect them to be able and willing to act as a positive role
model. And third, they have to be willing and able to develop others.
Let me tell you a little more about each of these characteristics,"
Brennan said.

"First, Diamond leaders need to be visionary and inspirational.
We look for people who can figure out where our business should
be heading, and can enlist others to get on board and make it happen.

"Second, if you want to be a leader around here, you have to be a role model. We've spent a lot of time on this one. Being a role model is like motherhood. Everybody agrees that it's important, but few people know how to do a good job of it."

"Unless I miss my guess, you have some pretty clear ideas about it at Diamond," Patricia laughed.

"Right," said Brennan. "We tell Diamond leaders that there are six keys to being an effective role model. One, spend your time on what you say is important. Two, ask a lot of questions — questions that point people in the right direction, help them develop their critical thinking skills and help them articulate what they already know. Three, use both your public and private communications to reinforce the Diamond Way. Four, remain cool and calm. Make sure you use the Diamond guiding principles to guide your actions during problems and crises. Five, reward behavior that is consistent with the Diamond Way. Six, redirect behavior that is inconsistent with the Diamond Way.

"When someone is promoted to his or her first leadership position, we give them a laminated card with these six keys on it. Most people carry it with them until it becomes second nature. Here, let me show you mine." Brennan reached into his wallet and pulled out a dog-eared card that looked like this.

BEING A DIAMOND ROLE MODEL

Focus on what's important

Ask lots of questions

Always reinforce the Diamond Way

Be calm

Reward the good

Change the not so good

"Finally, if you're going to be an effective Diamond leader, you must be willing and able to develop others for leadership positions. We want our leaders to be the kind of people who have the self-confidence to prepare others to take their job. A lot of leadership lessons are learned the hard way — through experience. However, we have found that leaders can accelerate others' learning by sharing their experiences — both good and bad. Our leaders are not afraid to admit their mistakes and tell people what they learned from them.

"If I sound a little intense on this subject, it's because I am," Brennan said. "In my opinion, our continued success as an organization has a lot to do with our ability to create the next and future generations of leaders — and to know when to step aside and let them take charge."

Patricia's Notes

COMMITMENT

- Commitment begins with the Selection process. High performing organizations actively recruit the type of people who will be a good fit.

- High performing organizations use Orientation as a commitment-building tool. Senior managers play a significant role in the Orientation process.

- Training programs not only teach skills, but also focus on how to apply the skills in a manner consistent with the organization's Mission and Guiding Pprinciples.

- Reward Systems are designed to foster commitment by rewarding the type of behavior that is consistent with the organization's Mission and Guiding Principles.

- Reward Systems focus on more than money. They are based on the idea that everyone wants to be appreciated. People continue to do the things for which they get rewarded. Words of encouragement and pats on the back are the keys to effective rewards.

- All members of high performing organizations demonstrate Leadership by helping one another and exemplifying high commitment.

- Formal leaders must be highly effective people:

  - Personal integrity

  - Personal responsibility

  - Empathy

  - Adaptability

  - Good communication skills

  - Appropriately ambitious

- Additional Leadership skills:

  - Vision — the ability to figure out where the organization should be going, and to enlist others in getting there

  - Role Modeling — leaders exemplify commitment in these ways:

    · Spend their time on what they say is important

    · Ask a lot of questions:

      - To point people in the right direction

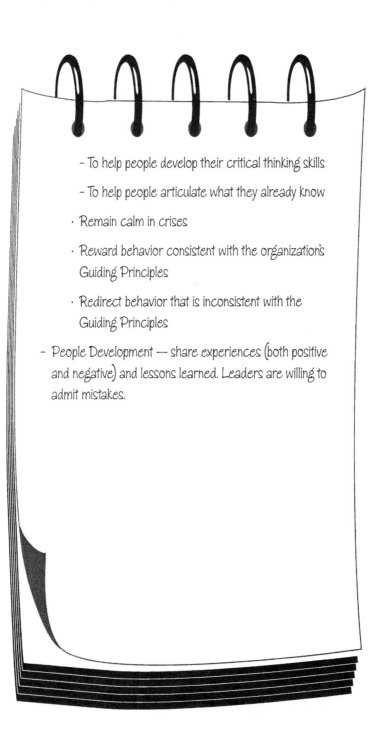

- To help people develop their critical thinking skills

- To help people articulate what they already know

· Remain calm in crises

· Reward behavior consistent with the organization's Guiding Principles

· Redirect behavior that is inconsistent with the Guiding Principles

- People Development — share experiences (both positive and negative) and lessons learned. Leaders are willing to admit mistakes.

Execution

The Spirit of
Operational Excellence

"You know, it sounds as if you spend a lot of your time focusing on the soft things around here," Patricia said. "Mission, guiding principles, learning, rewards, leadership. What about the hard stuff? You know: strategy, sales, distribution."

They were sitting in Brennan's office late on a Friday afternoon. Patricia had been reviewing her notes and was feeling a bit uncomfortable, as she hadn't yet uncovered any of Diamond's successful business practices and processes — at least not the ones she had always thought were critical to profitability.

"Well, for one thing," Brennan began. "I believe that the soft stuff is hard."

By now Brennan recognized that when Patricia screwed up her nose, she was thinking about what he said.

"The soft stuff is hard," she repeated. "Do you mean hard, difficult;

or that it is a hard business process?"

"Good question. And the answer is 'both.' The soft stuff is very difficult. It takes time and patience, and it's not what they teach you in business school. On the other hand, I believe that things many people think of as 'soft' are anything but. If you don't pay attention to developing the first two factors, clarity of purpose and the commitment of the people around you, you're not going to succeed — in business or in life.

"On the other hand, if you pay attention to only the soft side, you are not going to succeed either. That's where Execution comes in. When we talk about Execution around here, we are talking about operational excellence," Brennan said.

"Now we're getting somewhere," Patricia thought. "Operational excellence is a good start."

"What does operational excellence mean at Diamond?" she asked.

"For us, it means doing a good job of executing the things that matter," Brennan said.

"I'm sorry, I just don't get it," Patricia said. "Diamond is one of the most respected companies in the world, and you're telling me that your secret is 'executing the things that matter.' Well, doesn't every company try to do that?"

CHAPTER 17

Brennan smiled. "Yes, I guess they do. However, I never said our approach to operational excellence is a secret. I just said that it is one of the keys to our success."

Patricia looked a bit skeptical but decided to press on. "Tell me more."

"OK, " said Brennan. "But I think Helen is the best person to explain the Diamond approach to operational excellence. Why don't you take the weekend and think about what you've seen here so far, and then come back on Monday to meet with her? She is the COO after all. These 'hard things' are her bailiwick. I'm the 'soft stuff guy,' remember?"

Patricia smiled.

"Only joking," said Brennan. "I *am* the soft stuff guy around here. In fact, I often refer to myself as Diamond's CSO, not CEO."

"CSO?"

"Chief Spiritual Officer," Brennan said.

"Chief Spiritual Officer," Patricia repeated. "I can see how that fits you. I like it."

"I can't take credit for it," said Brennan. "I kind of borrowed it from Ken Blanchard."

"The *One Minute Manager* guy?" asked Patricia.

"Yes."

"Aren't those storybooks kind of corny?" said Patricia.

"Depends on how you look at it," said Brennan. "I find the approach to be elegantly simple. Stories are a powerful way of getting a message across. Good storytellers are able to find the essence of complex subjects and explain it in a simple, straightforward and entertaining way. Most of the executives I know would rather spend an hour or two reading a short, easy-to-understand book than plowing through an academic tome on the same subject."

"Makes sense, I guess," said Patricia. "I have to get going. Care if I come back and talk to you more about execution, Diamond style?"

"Of course," he said. "I enjoy our chats."

Brennan spent another half-hour cleaning up paperwork and went home to his family. This was going to be a special weekend. His daughter, Katie, was playing in the state championship field hockey game on Saturday, and he didn't want to miss it.

Strategic Metrics
for Execution

"You've been spending quite a bit of time around here. You must like us," Helen said. It was Monday morning and she and Patricia were sitting at the conference table in Helen's office.

"I do," said Patricia. "Brennan is a fascinating person. I've enjoyed listening to him and learning about his ideas. Does he really practice what he preaches?"

"Sure does," said Helen. "That's why Diamond is where it is today."

"He said to talk to you about the 'hard stuff '— like your approach to Execution, the mainstay of which is operational excellence."

Helen smiled. "That's my job. I'm the Chief Operating Officer, and I'm proud to say that we excel at operational excellence here at Diamond. The keys to our success are our planning and control systems. What can I tell you about them?"

"I don't mean to sound skeptical," Patricia began. "But don't all companies have planning and control systems? If I remember my Business 101 course, planning, organizing and controlling are the key elements of any business. I don't understand how something so basic can be a competitive advantage for you."

"Simple," Helen said. "We are serious about them. We don't just pay lip service to the concepts. We use them to run our business on a day-to-day basis. For example, every company has a strategic plan. People spend a lot of time creating these elaborate works of fiction...."

"Fiction!?" Patricia interrupted.

"Yes, fiction," Helen said. "After hours of writing and rewriting, these documents are beautifully bound and then put on a shelf somewhere. They're fiction in many companies because they bear absolutely no resemblance to what actually happens. Often nobody even reads them.

"It's a shame, too, because people spend a lot of time and energy writing them. Kind of reminds me of something my husband said when he was finishing his Ph.D. dissertation."

"What was that?" Patricia asked.

"He said, 'You know, honey, I had a painful realization today. I'm sweating bullets writing this thing that only five people will ever read — you, my mother and the three people on my committee.'

CHAPTER 18

I felt sorry for him because he probably was right. I feel sorry for
the people who write the strategic plans for a lot of companies, too.
I'm sure a lot of them feel the same way," Helen said.

"Enough of that stuff," she continued. "Let me tell you how we
approach strategy at Diamond. Remember when I told you about
our mission?" Helen asked.

"Yes."

"Our strategic plan provides the direction for all areas of the
business for the short and medium term. It flows from our mission.
The Diamond plan is really a compilation of our three operating
divisions' plans.

"These annual business plans are our bible. Our people live and
die by them. We have quarterly reviews to determine how well we
are doing at meeting our targets. We make adjustments — up and
down — as we go along.

"I believe the main reason we are successful is that we do an
excellent job of planning, but we do an even better job of tracking
our performance against our plans and making adjustments as we go."

"So you believe that Diamond is successful because you use the
Diamond mission to set your strategic direction," Patricia said. "You
use the strategic direction to develop detailed annual business plans;
and then you track your performance against the plan."

"Couldn't have said it better myself," said Helen.

"This sounds like déjà vu," said Patricia. "Juan has already told me how Diamond creates its annual business plans. I thought strategic planning was part of Clarity. Now we're talking about it as part of Execution."

"That's because there is some overlap," Helen explained. "Strategic planning is a big part of both Clarity and Execution. Our strategies are what we use to make our mission real. On the other hand, we have to execute these strategies if we are going to be successful. To execute our strategies, we have to develop metrics for each of them and then measure how well we're doing."

"That makes sense," said Patricia.

The Metrics
of Success

"So far, we've only touched on one aspect of the Execution factor. Yes, we have excellent planning processes, but the plans wouldn't be worth the paper they're written on if we didn't have good control systems to work with them," Helen said.

"Our control systems begin with our mission elements," she continued. "Do you remember what they are?"

"Hold on for just a second," said Patricia. "I'll find them in my notes. Here they are: product and service quality, customer satisfaction and financial performance."

"Good," Helen said. "We keep metrics on each of them, as well as on supplier performance and employee satisfaction."

"Everything ties together, doesn't it?" Patricia said.

"We think it does. Let me tell you a little about each of them," Helen said.

"Our product quality and service metrics measure our performance against what our customers have told us is most important to them. We use some pretty sophisticated sampling systems when it comes to these metrics. We go well beyond what many companies would deem significant.

"If we could, we would do quality checks on 100 percent of our goods and services. We don't for two reasons. First, it's just too expensive; and second, we are confident we have a culture of quality around here. We strive to build it, not inspect it, into our products and services.

"Whenever it's practical, we express our quality and service performance in actual numbers, not as a percentage. A 97 percent or even a 99 percent quality and service rate sounds good. In reality though, it gives us a false sense of security. We want 100 percent quality on goods and services. We find it's easier to achieve that if we report absolute numbers of quality and service problems — then make sure every problem gets resolved."

"Can you give me an example of an absolute number?" Patricia asked.

"Sure," Helen answered. "Let's say we achieve 99.998 percent quality. In absolute numbers, that translates to two defective products per 10,000. This doesn't sound like such a big deal — unless you're one of the two customers who got the defective products. So, whenever possible, we track quality in terms of actual numbers and make sure the problems we identify receive prompt corrective action."

"OK. Great," said Patricia. "How about your supplier metrics?"

"Our supplier metrics help us assess our product and service performance. They are a combination of hard data like 'purchased materials rejected' and 'on-time delivery of purchased materials,' as well as soft measures like our satisfaction with our suppliers' responsiveness to our needs. We measure these on a regular basis. We periodically audit our suppliers' processes so we can be confident in their ability to deliver what they promise. While cost is a consideration, it is only one of several metrics we use to assess our suppliers."

"Hold on a second, I need to finish up my notes," Patricia said.

Helen waited for Patricia, and then continued.

"Next is customer satisfaction. Our product quality and service metrics address this somewhat, but we really want to focus on how well we are meeting our customers' needs.

"We believe that our customers are the final arbiters of quality when it comes to product and service delivery. So we do extensive research to identify the things that are most important to them. In this way, we can be pretty confident that our metrics are measuring the right things.

"When it comes to customer satisfaction, we use both hard and soft measures. We gather data on how satisfied our customers are with our products and services, as well as their perceived value of what we offer. We use a variety of data-gathering techniques: telephone surveys, mail surveys and focus groups. Once we have the data, we roll it up into an overall customer satisfaction index.

"Finally, because we're in business to make a profit and create shareholder value, we measure our financial performance, too. We've identified a few key metrics that we think give us a pretty accurate picture of our financial performance. They're a mix of the short and long term, and they're consistent across all of our divisions. In this way, we collect and analyze the same information in the same way. Everybody is on the same page. We use return on equity as a summary statistic for all of our financial measures.

"We also collect and analyze information on a common set of operational measures. We consider our performance in these areas as part of our overall financial performance. Our operational metrics are designed to measure the things that tell us how well we are executing our strategies. For example, one of them is 'value added per employee.' We apply these measures to all of our divisions as well as to Diamond as a whole. That way, we can compare apples with apples. Most important, we use them to help us understand the root cause of problems and prevent them from recurring in the future.

"Still with me?" Helen asked.

Patricia nodded as she scribbled away.

"In addition to product and service quality, customer satisfaction and financial performance, we are concerned about employee satisfaction. We have developed a Guiding Principles Survey that is our primary means of measuring our employee satisfaction. It is based on the Diamond guiding principles, and provides us with a wealth of information on how well our employees think we are doing at living our values, which define the Diamond culture. The survey is anonymous and we get a phenomenal return rate. The response rate on our last Guiding Principles Survey was over 93 percent.

"We also keep track of things like voluntary turnover, absenteeism, requests for transfers and stress-related illnesses. We roll up all of these things in an overall employee satisfaction index, similar to our customer satisfaction index.

"So you see, we measure both the soft and hard sides of the business. We have well-developed metrics to measure the things we think are indicative of how well we are doing in executing what is important to our success," Helen finished.

"You sure do," Patricia agreed.

Managing the White Space

"Let's talk about another important part of the Execution factor: structure," Helen said.

"Organizations come with a built-in paradox. The reason we have organizations in the first place is that no one person or small group of people can do everything necessary to keep a company in business. So we have to find a way to divide up the work. Organizational theory experts call this 'differentiation.' With me so far?"

Patricia nodded.

"Good, but differentiation creates a huge issue: integration. Once you've broken down an organization into its component parts, you have to figure out how those parts are going to work together. The trick is to manage the white spaces on the organization chart — the spaces between the boxes."

"So what you're saying is that all organizations must find some way to divide up the work, and then figure out some way to make all the parts work together," Patricia said.

"Yes. And that is easier said than done," Helen replied. "You write about businesses. I'm sure you hear stories about turf wars in companies all the time. From the look on your face, I know you do.

"Turf wars are a prime example of poor integration. Most people think they exist because a few people just can't get along. That may be partially true. However, the biggest reason turf wars exist is that organizations don't create enough coordinating mechanisms to manage the white spaces on their organization charts."

"What do you mean by coordinating mechanisms?" Patricia asked.

"Here's an example. In many companies, marketing and production don't get along. Why is this? If you talk to the marketing people, most often they'll tell you that the production people are 'inflexible.' If you talk to the production people, they'll tell you that the marketing people live in a dream world, expecting them to be able to change everything on a whim.

"Let's look at the jobs these people have and the worlds they live in. If you're in marketing, you live and die with the customer. If you have orange widgets and all of a sudden the customer wants pink widgets, you know that you had better come up with some pink widgets pretty quickly or you're going to lose a lot of market share.

"Now let's look at this situation from a production perspective. You're happy making orange widgets. You've got your lines set up and dialed in. You can crank out orange widgets better than anybody. Every year you get more and more efficient. You're good at making orange widgets. You like making orange widgets.

"All of a sudden, here come the marketing people, and they want pink widgets. Well, pink widgets are a little harder to make because the pink pigment doesn't seem to work as well with your equipment as the orange pigment did. And besides that, marketing didn't tell you that their marketing research has shown that people like their widgets three millimeters bigger than the old widgets. It kind of slipped their mind. Besides, how could three teeny millimeters cause you any problems, anyway?

"You can guess what happens. Production takes too long to retool to make the larger pink widgets. By that time all your competitors have their larger pink widgets on the market and your sales are way below forecast.

"Marketing blames production for being unresponsive to changing market conditions. Production blames marketing for providing incomplete information and setting an unrealistic launch schedule. Both sides point fingers and the business suffers."

"Does that kind of stuff really happen?" asked Patricia.

"About a thousand times a day in companies all over the country," Helen answered.

"How do you prevent it from happening here?"

"Coordinating mechanisms."

"Ah, those," said Patricia.

"Yes, those."

"How do you use coordinating mechanisms at Diamond? I'm sure you do, or you wouldn't have told me the widget story."

"We do," Helen said. "In most cases they prevent white-space problems, but white-space problems are persistent; even we have them from time to time.

"We call our coordinating mechanisms 'cross-functional teams.' They are designed to stop our white-space problems before they start. These teams have participation from every link in the supply chain: marketing, sales, product development, production, distribution. Probably the best way to explain it to you is to let you meet some of the people involved with one of our product development teams."

Helen picked up her Palm Pilot and fiddled with the stylus. "Good. One of them is meeting this afternoon at 1 o'clock.

"Why don't you take some time to get caught up on your notes?

CHAPTER 20

That will give me a chance to take care of some of these e-mails that have been coming in over the past hour. We'll get a quick bite in the cafeteria at 12:30, and then go over to the meeting. I won't be able to stay, but I'll introduce you to the team. They're nice people and they won't mind if you sit in and observe. I'll ask Paul to answer any questions you might have."

"OK," said Patricia as she gathered her things to leave.

Patricia's Notes

EXECUTION

- Execution = Operational Excellence

- Operational Excellence is the result of excellent Planning and Control Systems.

- Control Systems are built around the Mission Elements. Control Systems focus on measuring performance against the things identified as important to the organization.

- In this case, Control Systems focus on:
  - Quality
  - Customer Satisfaction
  - Financial Performance
  - Supplier Performance
  - Employee Satisfaction

- Organizational Structure is another key to execution.

  - Coordinating Mechanisms help manage the white spaces on an organization chart.

    - Cross-functional Teams are a good example of Coordinating Mechanisms.

Relationships

Dancing Backward, Gracefully

Patricia and Brennan were sitting in Brennan's office late the next afternoon. She had just finished recapping what she had learned about Diamond's approach to Execution.

"Well, Patricia," said Brennan. "I hope you've learned a lot about Diamond over the past few weeks. We don't claim to have all the answers, but we think we have figured out a few things."

"I've enjoyed the time I've spent here at Diamond," Patricia said. "Everybody has been so open and forthcoming. A lot of companies don't like to share the kind of information you've shared with me, you know."

"We don't mind sharing how we do things around here. As I've told you, I don't think we do anything that's particularly different or innovative. We're just committed to the things we've decided to do. Our competitive advantage isn't a unique approach to managing our business. It's our willingness to stick to what we know works."

Brennan leaned forward and continued. "Many leaders are looking for the quick fix and tend to buy into every new fad that comes along. But if you're clear on where you're going, if you can get people behind your plan and moving in the right direction, if you execute well on your goals and objectives, and if you build the right relationships, you can't help but be successful."

"I guess there's just one thing left for us to discuss, the fourth quadrant on your coaster — Relationships," Patricia said.

"Well, as you probably would guess by now, we don't do anything complicated there, either. Let's get a cup of coffee, and I'll tell you about it."

After they settled in at a corner table in the cafeteria, Brennan began to discuss Diamond's approach to what he called "our world."

"Our world, just like any company's world, is pretty complicated," he said. "Many organizations miss this point. They tend to focus inward exclusively. Our first three secrets — Clarity, Commitment and Execution — have an internal focus. They are designed to help us improve what we do internally.

"But we've found that too much of an internal focus is dangerous. There's a big world out there, and we have to pay attention to what's going on in it if we are going to succeed in the long run.

If we don't focus externally, we can get blind-sided by change. We've found that if we build strong relationships with important people and groups outside of Diamond, we are less likely to find ourselves in a position of being surprised by changes outside of our control.

"There are all sorts of people and organizations outside of Diamond with whom we need to build and maintain solid relationships. One way we may be unique is that at Diamond, we believe the same principles apply to dealing with any outside constituency. We apply these principles to our relationships with customers, suppliers, business partners, investors, government regulators, the communities in which we operate — anyone outside of Diamond who has a stake in what we do."

"You treat all those different groups the same?" Patricia asked, raising her eyebrows.

"No, not the same," Brennan said. "But we apply the same set of principles to all of them."

"You've got my attention," said Patricia. "What are those principles? I'm all ears — and ready to write." She held up her pen.

"OK. Since you're ready I won't keep you in suspense. But I have to warn you, you might find these principles fairly pedestrian," Brennan said.

"Let me be the judge of that," Patricia said.

Brennan took a deep breath, leaned back in his chair and launched in.

"We believe that any group or organization that has a stake in what we do should be treated as a valued partner. We can't be successful without these constituencies, so we feel it's in our best interest to develop partnership relationships with them."

"How do you do that?" Patricia asked.

"It's pretty simple," said Brennan. "Early on, we spent a good deal of time deciding what makes for a solid partnership. We decided that good partnerships have five things in common. First, they are long term. Second, they are grounded in truth and trust. Third, they are mutually beneficial. Fourth, they are balanced. Fifth, they are graceful."

"Graceful!?" Patricia blurted.

"Yes, graceful," Brennan said. "Let me tell you what I mean. I think Fred Astaire and Ginger Rogers defined grace on the dance floor. When you watched them dance, it seemed effortless. They seemed to anticipate each other's moves and — when they needed to — compensate for each other. We think that this is part of an effective business partnership. We focus on anticipating the needs of our partners.

"As they say, 'Fred danced beautifully, but Ginger did the same thing — backward and in high heels,'" he smiled. "We think we're successful because we're pretty good at dancing backward in high heels with our partners.

"We are fanatical about anticipating our customers' needs. We position ourselves as a supplier who will work with them to meet their needs and solve their problems. We do this because we know that without customers we are all lost.

"If the dot-com implosion has taught us anything, it's that the best business plan and tons of financing are nothing without real customers who have a real demand for real products and services. We are successful because we provide our customers with the products and services they want and need, when they want and need them, sometimes even before they know they need them.

"This works both ways. Our customers have been willing to work with us, cutting us some slack in the infrequent times when we run into some extraordinary problem. It's just the nature of a good partnership.

"We extend the same courtesy to our suppliers. We realize they are in business too, and that they need to be profitable if they are going to be able to provide us with the goods and services we need to be successful. So we work with them to help them become more successful.

"Let me give you a concrete example. A couple of years ago, we had a supplier that developed a peculiar and somewhat baffling quality problem all of a sudden. We had worked with these guys for years. We trusted them when they told us that the problem had them stumped. We sent a couple of our engineers to work with them. Working together with the supplier's people, they identified the root cause and solved the problem in about a week.

"We could have said, 'It's your problem, fix it fast or lose our business.' But because we believe that good partnerships are graceful, meaning partners help compensate for each other's weaknesses, we didn't. It cost us very little to send those engineers down there. Not only did we solve our raw material quality problem, we strengthened our relationship with the supplier.

"Our overriding rule of relationship management is, 'When dealing with a partner, always try to leave with a stronger relationship than when you arrived.' We're not looking for quantum leaps in the quality of relationships, just incremental improvements that make for strong, lasting partnerships."

"I see," said Patricia as she busily scribbled notes on her pad. "I got you off track a little. We started talking about Number Five before I gave you a chance to explain the first four to me."

Long-Term Partners:
Building Trust with Truth

"OK, I'll back up," Brennan said. Number One is 'long-term.' We believe that effective partnerships are lasting. We want to keep our customers for life. We want our suppliers to continue doing business with us. By definition, we have long-term relationships with our regulators, so we try to help them be effective.

"Finally, when we set up shop in a community, we expect to stay there for a long time. Our goal is to become valued members of the communities where we do business. So we invest in them. We encourage our employees to become active in the community. We adopt schools. We supply tutors, especially in math and science. We support Junior Achievement. We donate obsolete computers and other office equipment to the local Boys and Girls Clubs. We get active in the local Chamber of Commerce.

"We do these things because we believe that a healthy community is in our best interest. If the schools are good and the communities in which we operate are pleasant places to live, we can attract the kind of employees we need to be successful.

"On the other hand, we believe that we have an obligation to give something back to our communities. They trust us to operate there. We need to repay that trust."

"You're serious about this stuff, aren't you?"

"Yes," said Brennan. "I sometimes get a little carried away when I get going on our responsibility to our communities.

"On to Number Two: truth and trust," he said.

"On to number Two," Patricia nodded.

"To me this is a no-brainer," Brennan said. "All good relationships are based on truth and trust. The two go hand in hand. You can't trust me if you think I'm not truthful. And if I'm not truthful — just one time — you won't trust me. Trust is fragile. It takes a long time to build but only a minute to destroy. Once it's destroyed, it takes even longer to rebuild it.

"Several years ago, we appointed a new plant manager in one of our divisions. He found that we had misreported some of our lost-time accident statistics. When he figured this out, he notified OSHA immediately. They sent a few people over to question him and his people about what they had reported and why they were changing it now. Our people answered all of the questions, and OSHA went away happy. The plant manager told the division president that as they were leaving, one of the OSHA people said to him, 'You know, in all the years I've been in this business, I've never seen anyone turn themselves in to us. You guys are honorable people.'

"They've had that same inspector back on a number of occasions. He is always willing to cut them some slack. If he identifies an unsafe condition and we tell him we'll fix it, he believes us.

"This has carried over to our relationship with other regulators and other plants. We always do well on OSHA inspections. Mostly it's because we take our environmental health and safety responsibilities seriously, but in part I believe it's because we have built a trusting relationship with the agency. We have demonstrated our willingness to work with them as partners," Brennan concluded.

"So by coming clean with the agency on one thing, you can get away with cutting some corners on others?" Patricia asked.

"No," Brennan said. "That's not the point at all. We informed the agency of our honest mistake in reporting our lost-time accidents because it was the right thing to do. We were acting on our belief that we can build a strong, trusting partnership with our regulators by being truthful with them. Truth leads to trust. The inspector I was telling you about knows that we can be counted on to do what we say we'll do.

"We have a good relationship with this agency because of the trust we've built with them. But we have no illusions. We can destroy that trust in a split second if we don't keep our commitments."

"As usual, this is very interesting," said Patricia. "But I have to go now. May we pick this up tomorrow?"

"Tomorrow isn't good for me," said Brennan. "Why don't you speak with Helen? She had a lot to do with creating our outside relationships philosophy. Let me see if she is available."

Brennan picked up the phone and spoke with Helen's assistant. He put down the receiver. "She can have lunch with you tomorrow. Does that work for you?"

Patricia nodded.

"Good," said Brennan. "You'll probably learn more from her than you will from me, anyway."

Succeeding by Helping Others Succeed

At 12:30 p.m. the next day, Patricia and Helen were sitting down for lunch in the Diamond cafeteria.

"We could have gone out but I'm a little pressed for time today," Helen said.

"That's OK. I always like to eat here and observe the Diamond culture," Patricia said.

"Good, " said Helen. "I'm glad you like it here. "We're kind of proud of it. What are we talking about today?"

"The way Diamond handles external relationships," said Patricia. "Brennan and I covered the first two, long-term and trust and truth. We also covered the last one, graceful. He said you could cover the other two with me."

Helen smiled. "He did, did he? I can do that. Let's start with 'mutually beneficial.' To me, the notion of a mutually beneficial relationship is simple. Mutually beneficial relationships are based on the concept of win/win. In all of our relationships with our important outside constituencies, we attempt to create a situation in which neither we nor our partner feels taken advantage of.

"This cafeteria is a good example of a mutually beneficial relationship," she continued. "As you know, we're in an office park. It's not like being in the downtown area of a large city where people have any number of dining options open to them within a few blocks. If our people leave the building, they have to drive to a restaurant. Not only is it inconvenient for them, long lunches cut into productivity.

"A few years ago, we found that more people than usual were leaving the building for lunch. We did an informal survey and found that our employees felt that the quality of our cafeteria's food had deteriorated.

"We went to the vendor and they agreed. They told us that they had been hit with rising expenses. Salaries and benefits, as well as food costs, had risen dramatically over the previous 12 months. Because we subsidize the cafeteria, they felt they couldn't raise prices. Our contract locked them into a pricing structure. To keep their margins from disappearing completely, they had begun to cut some corners.

CHAPTER 23

"This got kicked up to me," Helen continued. "I met with the vendor's people and asked why they hadn't discussed these cost problems with us. They said that they were in the fourth year of a five-year contract and felt that we would not be interested in their problems.

"To make a long story short, we increased our subsidy of the cafeteria. This allowed the vendor to make some money. And it had a secondary effect. People started eating in the cafeteria again, which took less time away from their work. We started getting compliments about the improved quality of the food. Our people were happy. And we believe that happy people are more productive.

"The vendor was happy, too. We had enjoyed a good relationship with them for several years and we didn't want that to change. By working with the vendor and raising our subsidy, everybody concerned won. Our employees got what they wanted — a pleasant dining atmosphere with nutritious, tasty food at a reasonable price. The vendor met its own needs, making a profit. Diamond cemented the relationship with a vendor we know, like and trust. And as a bonus, we gained goodwill with our employees in addition to higher productivity, at least theoretically. Not only was this a win/win situation. It was a win/win/win."

"But it cost you more money to increase the subsidy," Patricia said.

"Yes it did," said Helen. "But we believe the increase in the subsidy, which was modest anyway, is more than offset by the gains I just mentioned.

"I don't mean to sound as if we throw money at every vendor who complains of rising costs. We'd be out of business if we did. In this case, though, we believe that the cost involved was justified by the returns.

"Ultimately, we believe that it is in our best interests for us to help our suppliers become more successful. When they're successful, we benefit. We benefit because their goods and services are more likely to meet our standards. We don't want to pay them more than we need to, but we find that successful suppliers are consistently good suppliers, and that's what we need to run this business."

Balancing the Seesaw
of Cost and Quality

"Let's move on to the idea of balance," Helen said.

"Yes, I'm interested to learn what balance means in the context of relationships," said Patricia.

"What comes to mind when you hear the word balance?" Helen asked.

Patricia thought for a second. "A seesaw."

"Good. Let's use that example. If you think about it, seesaws are most often out of balance. One person is at the top, and the other person is at the bottom. It takes a lot of work and effort from both parties to hold a seesaw in balance, where everything is level.

"That's the way we think about balance in our relationships with our outside constituencies. Take customers for example. In general, what do customers want?"

"You mean Diamond's customers?" Patricia asked.

"No, customers in general," Helen said.

"Well, I guess they want quality goods and services at a cheap price," Patricia said.

"Close," Helen said. "We find that most customers want quality goods and services, at a *reasonable* price. People are willing to pay for quality. They just don't want to overpay. In our experience, customers want value. Value is decided by a simple equation: what you got, divided by what it cost you."

Patricia looked puzzled.

Helen picked up a pad. "Here, let me draw it for you."

When she turned the pad around, Patricia saw:

<u>GOT</u>
COST

Helen continued, "Most people are willing to pay a little more for a product or service that they believe gives them a little more than the basics. And when they prefer to pay less, they realize that they are not going to get as much. Each person has his or her own got/cost equation for most of the items they purchase.

"Let's use an example. What kind of car do you drive?"

"A Jeep Cherokee," said Patricia.

"Why do you have a Cherokee instead of a Grand Cherokee?" Helen asked.

"Because the Cherokee does what I want it to do, and it costs a lot less." Patricia smiled.

"OK, I get it," Patricia continued. "I could get something more if I bought a Grand Cherokee, but what I would get by buying a Grand Cherokee isn't worth the cost to me. The equation doesn't add up. I bought the Cherokee because what I got makes it worth the cost to me of buying it."

"That's right," said Helen. "In other words, buying the Cherokee created a sense of balance for you. You balanced the got/cost ratio to your satisfaction."

"Exactly," Patricia said.

"It works that way with all customer relationships. A lot of companies that compete with our Industrial Division treat their product as a commodity and price it as such. We have products similar to those of our competitors, but our Industrial Division has a large Product Application Department. This department's sole reason for existence is to help our customers use our products. We have technical specialists on call for our customers. They assist them in applying our products to their unique situations. As a result, we charge more for our products than some of our competitors do.

"And do you know what? Our customers tell us they are glad to pay it. They tell us our technical service enables them to be more efficient, and they are willing to pay our higher prices for increased efficiency and productivity.

"In the end, it's all about balance. In our customers' minds, our world-class service offsets our higher product costs. On balance, they are confident they come out ahead by buying from us."

Patricia's Notes

RELATIONSHIPS

- Important outside constituencies:
    - Customers
    - Suppliers
    - Business Partners
    - Investors
    - Government Regulators
    - Communities

- Organizations must create effective partnerships with outside constituencies. Effective partnerships are:
    - Long-term
    - Grounded in truth and trust
    - Mutually beneficial
    - Balanced (good Got/Cost relationship for all sides)
    - Graceful

- When dealing with a partner, always do everything you can to leave with a stronger relationship than when you arrived.

The End...And
A New Beginning

Fad Surfing
and the Program Trap

"Well, Patricia," said Brennan the next morning. "You've been with us for quite a while now. I hope you've gathered the material you need for your article." They were sitting at the conference table in Brennan's office.

"It's been interesting," Patricia answered. "I appreciate your openness. You gave me access to everyone in Diamond who I wanted to see. The simplicity of the concepts you used to build Diamond was most interesting to me. I'll go as far as saying that your concepts are elegant in their simplicity."

"Thanks, but don't forget breadth," Brennan laughed. "Breadth and simplicity are our watchwords around here."

"I buy that," said Patricia. "I amend my statement to say that the Diamond keys to success are elegant in their simplicity and comprehensiveness."

"Thanks," said Brennan. "I couldn't have said it better myself."

"You know, I like it so much, I think I'll use it as my lead. 'Diamond Inc., under the leadership of Brennan Newell, is the model of breadth and simplicity.' What do you think?" she asked.

"Not bad," said Brennan.

"I really like the way you have combined those two potentially contradictory concepts," Patricia said. "There are a lot of people who think it's impossible to be both simple and comprehensive or all-encompassing at the same time."

"That's why you see so many companies running into what I call the program trap," said Brennan.

Patricia raised her eyebrows.

"What I mean is that many companies jump on all of the latest fads that come along. All fads come with programs — usually designed by consultants — that promise to solve all of your problems," Brennan continued.

"If you're not careful, you'll end up with a bunch of programs. Most of them will have some things in common. However, by their very nature, programs use different words for the same concepts. This might help the consulting companies sell their services and materials, but it confuses most people in their client companies.

"Our Clarity, Commitment, Execution, Relationships model

helps us avoid this problem. When we see the latest 'gotta have' program, we ask how it fits with one of our four factors. If it doesn't fit, we question ourselves first. We ask, 'Is our model broad enough?' To date, we haven't found anything that has prompted us to add another element to the model. We might someday. We just haven't as yet.

"If a program fits with one of the factors in our model, we ask, 'Is it really any different from what we are doing already?' Most often the answer is 'no.' In this case, we say, 'Thanks, but no thanks,' and go on our way.

"Occasionally, we find something that fits with our model and is a departure from what we have been doing — a significantly better way of doing things. We jump on this and incorporate it into our arsenal.

"I'm not saying that we don't get swayed by a good sales pitch occasionally but by and large we avoid the program trap by sticking with our model, applying simple concepts well and throughout the entire company.

"I read a book called *Fad Surfing in the Boardroom* once. It did a much better job of explaining this problem than I am doing right now. I bought it and gave it to all of our senior executives and board members. When we find ourselves considering a new initiative of any kind, someone always asks, 'Is this something that fits for us, or are we just fad surfing here?' That question always brings a dose of reality to our conversations.

"In a long-winded way, I'm trying to tell you that while we are open to new ideas, we do a pretty good job of avoiding old ideas repackaged in a glitzy format. We focus broadly but we prefer simple approaches to our work," he finished.

"I understand," Patricia said. "Let me show you the outline of my article. I think you'll like it."

"OK," said Brennan. "But let's take a little break first. I'd like Helen to see this too."

Outlining Breadth
and Simplicity

Fifteen minutes later, Brennan, Helen and Patricia were back at the conference table in Brennan's office. Brennan's assistant had thoughtfully provided a bottle of water for each of them. Patricia reached into her briefcase and pulled out three copies of her outline.

"Before I give you this outline, I want you to know that I've learned a lot in the time that I've spent here," she said. "The concept of combining seemingly disparate ideas such as breadth and simplicity is one of your ideas that has made a big impact on me. So much so, that I've tried to apply it to this article. I really tried to be both broad and simple at the same time. You can tell me if I've been successful."

Brennan and Helen couldn't help but smiling when they heard this.

Brennan said, "Patricia, if you really were able to be both broad and simple in this article, I'm sure it will be a masterpiece. Now let's take a look at your outline."

Patricia handed a copy of the outline to both of them with a somewhat expectant look on her face. Brennan and Helen both reached for their reading glasses and began scanning the outline. It looked like this.

Diamond Inc.

A Study in Breadth and Simplicity

1. Four Factor Model — broad but simple concepts
2. Secret is in the application of the ideas, not the ideas themselves
3. Factors include: Clarity, Commitment, Execution, Relationships
4. Clarity:
   a. Mission
   b. Mission Elements
   c. Values
   d. Business Plans
   e. Individual Objectives
5. Commitment
   a. Selection
   b. Orientation

---

CHAPTER 26

c. Training

d. Reward Systems

e. Leadership

6. Execution

    a. Operational Excellence

    b. Planning Systems

    c. Control Systems

    d. Coordinating Mechanisms

7. Relationships

    a. Who?

        i. Customers

        ii. Suppliers

        iii. Regulators

        iv. Communities

    b. How?

        i. Partnerships

            a. Long-term

            b. Truth and trust

            c. Mutually beneficial

            d. Balanced

            e. Graceful

"No fads. Stick to the model. Never forget breadth and simplicity. Looks good to me," said Helen.

"Looks *great* to me," said Brennan. "Patricia, you've done a great job of capturing the spirit of the way we try to operate around here. I'll look forward to seeing the article in print."

"Thanks," said Patricia. "I've enjoyed learning about Diamond and how one can think both broadly and simply at the same time. I hope the article does Diamond justice."

"I'm sure it will," said Brennan. "If you need any clarification as you write, please don't hesitate to call us."

"I won't," said Patricia as she gathered her things and left.

CHAPTER 27

Celebrating Documented Success

Three months later, Patricia's article, with Brennan and Helen on the magazine cover, hit the newsstands. Brennan had insisted that Helen be pictured with him. As he told anyone who would listen, "Helen and I are a team. She deserves as much credit for Diamond's success as I do."

Diamond purchased reprints of the article — complete with the color cover — for every Diamond employee. The text of the article was posted on the Diamond Web site.

"It's been quite a ride, Helen. I'm glad you were at my side for it. I think it's time we took the next step," said Brennan.

A few days later, the following letter from Brennan was posted on the Diamond intranet.

Dear Diamond Colleague:

Today is a proud day for Diamond. Being featured in a national business publication is quite an honor. I'm proud of you for making it happen. The article may feature me, but the credit for our success rightfully belongs to you. Thank you for all of your hard work and dedication. But as we all know, in today's business world the question is, "What have you done for me lately?" So, while we should take some time to enjoy our moment in the sun, we still need to be thinking about the future.

At yesterday's meeting, our Board of Directors accepted my resignation as CEO of Diamond. I will remain on as Chairman of the Board through the next calendar year. The Board also unanimously passed a resolution appointing Helen Yee as my successor as CEO.

Helen has been an invaluable part of the Diamond Leadership Team for the past 10 years. She is as responsible for our success as anyone. She has displayed the leadership necessary to take Diamond forward. I could not be leaving the company in better hands.

I'm sure that you will do your best to assist Helen in the continued growth of our company. After all, you're Diamond people — the experts at the Diamond Way. Thank you for the support you have given me these past 10 years. I know that Helen can count on you too.

Brennan Newell, CEO

Advice for the Road Ahead

A month later, Helen was formally introduced as the Diamond CEO designate at the Diamond annual shareholder meeting. After acknowledging the audience's applause, she began.

> "I've been proud to work with Brennan Newell these past 10 years. Under his leadership, Diamond has grown and prospered. He's leaving me some big shoes to fill.
>
> "But Brennan is also leaving me the secret of his success and a guide for leading Diamond into the future. Only, the secret is no secret. In fact, we shared it with the world recently.
>
> "For those of you who haven't read the article, the Diamond secret to success is 'breadth and simplicity.' We achieved the success we enjoyed over the past 10 years because we have embraced these two potentially conflicting concepts.

"We created a Four Factor Model that is the essence of breadth and simplicity. We've built this company on the notion that we must:

- *Have a clarity of purpose and direction.*
- *Obtain the sincere commitment of every member of Diamond Inc.*
- *Skillfully execute the things that matter.*
- *And build and maintain mutually beneficial relationships with important Diamond constituencies.*

"These are the keys to our success. Yes, they are broad and cover the entire business landscape. However, they are simple concepts, easy to understand and apply. And it's the consistent application of these concepts that accounts for our success. That's why we didn't worry about sharing them with the world.

"It was relatively easy to develop and espouse these concepts, but it took persistence, dedication and courage to stick with them and tie everything we do to them.

"Brennan Newell is the embodiment of persistence, dedication and courage. Under his leadership, Diamond people have come to embody these same characteristics. So in many ways, my job is simple: Get out of the way

and continue to let Diamond people apply our simple but broad keys to success.

"And that's exactly what I'm planning to do."

Helen sat down to thunderous applause, which resounded not only in the auditorium where she was speaking, but also in Diamond meeting and conference rooms around the world where the meeting was being broadcast live via closed circuit television.

As they were leaving the stage, Brennan reached into his pocket. He pulled out the laminated coaster Helen had given him more than 10 years ago.

He pressed it into her hand. "This is yours now. I'm going to give you unsolicited advice only once. Keep this on your desk. When you are faced with a tough decision, look to it for guidance."

"I'll do that," she said. "Thanks, Brennan."

"No. Thank you. You believed in my ideas, and together we built this company into what it is today. I couldn't have done it without you. Remember: breadth and simplicity."

"What have I gotten myself into now?" Helen thought to herself.

Later that day, she reached into her pocket and found the coaster. Touching it was reassuring. "Clarity, Commitment, Execution and Relationships. I can handle that."

She smiled at the future.

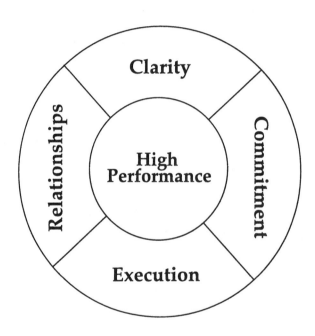

This book has provided you with some excellent insights into what it takes to build and sustain a high performing organization. Bud Bilanich's four secrets, Clarity, Commitment, Execution and Relationships, are broad enough to cover the complexities of today's tough business climate, but simple enough to be understood and used by anyone.

As good as these secrets are, if you don't each take personal responsibility for implementing them, you won't get far in building a high performing organization. Blame, complaining and procrastination will undoubtedly be your worst enemies, if they are not already. That's why I wrote *QBQ! The Question Behind the Question: Practicing Personal Accountability in Business and Life,* a guide to eliminating these destructive forces — in our organizations and our personal lives.

Bud asked me to identify some QBQs (Questions Behind the
Question) to help you apply the four secrets. Listed below are
some questions that will help your organization make personal
accountability a core value. These QBQs will take you a long way
toward building an organization you are proud to call your own.

Clarity QBQs:

- How can I create and communicate a clear vision for the
  part of the business that I manage?
- What can I do to think more strategically every day?
- How can I define my values as a leader?
- What can I do to help others understand these values?
- How can I provide the people with whom I work, clear
  performance objectives that support these values?

Commitment QBQs:

- How can I create an atmosphere in which people feel
  included and valued?
- What can I do to ensure that everyone's voice is heard?
- How can I help my people succeed?
- How can I show people they're important to our success?
- How can I communicate better?

- What can I do today be a better leader?
- What can I do to maximize the talents of those who work with me?

Execution QBQs

- How can I help people learn from their mistakes?
- What can I do to ensure that people have the knowledge, skills and tools they need to be successful?
- How can I create a set of meaningful metrics for our work?
- What can I do to use these metrics to manage my part of the business more effectively?
- How can I create systems that will make our work more error-free?
- How can I help solve our problems?

Relationship QBQs

- How can I build better relationships with my customers?
- How can I increase the value my customers receive?
- How can I build better relationships with my suppliers?
- How can I make the regulators' jobs easier for them?
- What can I do to build strong relationships with the local community?

· A F T E R W O R D ·

At the end of *Four Secrets,* Bud points out that while the secrets are powerful in and of themselves, it takes "persistence, dedication and courage" to practice them all the time. These QBQs are a good starting point for your journey. If you ask the right questions of yourself, you can accomplish anything you set out to do — including building a truly high performing organization.

John Miller, author, QBQ! The Question Behind the Question: Practicing Personal Accountability in Business and in Life www.QBQ.com

My job as a consultant is to assist my clients in developing their organizations. Often, this involves teaching and coaching. Even though I am supposed to be the teacher in these engagements, I have learned so much from my clients that I sometimes wonder (only briefly) whether I should be paying them for the well-rounded business education I have received as a result of working with them.

As I have analyzed and reflected on what I've learned, I've come to realize that more than anything, strong organizations are built on the dual characteristics of breadth and simplicity. I've seen it over and over in successful organizations. The Four Factor Model of Clarity, Commitment, Execution and Relationships emerged from my work with companies of varying sizes in a number of different industries. Today, many companies are enjoying the success that results from using this simple model.

· AUTHOR'S NOTE ·

There is real power in the four factors of Clarity, Commitment, Execution and Relationships. These factors can unleash the potential of your organization. My purpose in writing this book is to present these concepts to you in an easy-to-use form, to suggest that you consider making them the foundation of your organization, and to provide you with some ideas for applying them in your situation.

Where do you go from here? I suggest these steps:

1. Think about how Clarity, Commitment, Execution and Relationships apply to your unique situation.

2. Identify the practices necessary to make these four factors come alive in your organization.

3. Put these practices to work. Nurture them and guard them. Be persistent, dedicated and courageous about applying them.

4. Watch your organization grow and prosper.

Bud Bilanich
Denver, CO

· ABOUT THE AUTHOR ·

BUD BILANICH, Ed.D.

D
r. Bilanich is President of the Organization Effectiveness Group, a consulting firm specializing in improving the effectiveness of individuals, teams and organizations. His unique ability to combine a thorough conceptual understanding of organization theory with a results-oriented, pragmatic approach to problem solving pays big dividends for his clients.

He has more than 25 years' experience in leadership development and organizational effectiveness. He consults with senior executives and line managers on leadership effectiveness issues, and the design and implementation of major strategic change initiatives. He is also an executive coach. His experience and maturity help clients grow in their personal and professional effectiveness.

Bud has trained thousands of salespeople, managers and executives. Recently he developed and implemented a Corporate University, including basic and advanced leadership programs, for a Fortune 500 company. He designed the highly acclaimed training programs, "Leadership in a Values Driven Organization" and "Superior Sales Management." Both are in use in more than 40 countries around the globe.

Bud is an internationally known speaker who brings an abundance of energy and wit to his keynotes. Audiences in North America, Latin America, Europe and Asia have benefited from his insight. He received an Ed.D. in Adult Education and Organization Behavior and Intervention from Harvard University. He is listed in *Who's Who in Global Business Leaders*. He is active in the National Speakers Association, the American Society for Training and Development and the International Coach Federation.

In addition to *Four Secrets of High Performing Organizations,* he is the author of two other books, both published by Front Row Press: *Supervisory Leadership and the New Factory* and *Using Values to Turn Vision into Reality.*

Bud Bilanich
The Organization Effectiveness Group
875 South Colorado Boulevard, #773
Denver, CO 80246
(303) 393-0446
(303) 393-0081 fax
www.oegconsulting.com
Bud.Bilanich@oegconsulting.com

Also Available from
Bud Bilanich
and The Organization Effectiveness Group

Additional copies of
Four Secrets of High Performing Organizations
A great gift for anyone in a leadership position.
Order any quantity direct.

The Four Secrets Organizational Audit
See how well your organization measures
up to the Four Secrets.

The Four Secrets Workshop
Delivered by Bud Bilanich
or a certified OEG consultant.

The Four Secrets Training System
Designed to be delivered by certified
in-house facilitators.

Keynote presentations by Bud Bilanich
There's nothing like a live presentation,
especially when the speaker is Bud Bilanich.
Meet Bud in person and treat your group to his
energy and passion for creating high
performing organizations.

For more information or to order any of these
products and services, contact us at:
The Organization Effectiveness Group
875 South Colorado Boulevard, # 773, Denver, CO 80246
(303) 393-0446 / (303) 393-0081 (fax)
E-mail: info@oegconsulting.com
Web site: www.oegconsulting.com

Additional Books By
Bud Bilanich

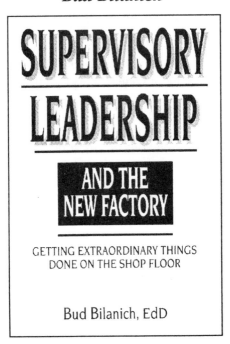

SUPERVISORY
LEADERSHIP

AND THE
NEW FACTORY

GETTING EXTRAORDINARY THINGS
DONE ON THE SHOP FLOOR

Bud Bilanich, EdD

Praise for Supervisory Leadership and the New Factory

"Dr. Bilanich has an uncommon grasp of what is needed by front line manufacturing leaders. This book is must reading for anyone interested in managing an effective manufacturing organization."

Tony Maddaluna, Vice President Manufacturing, Europe, Pfizer Inc

Praise for Using Values to turn Vision into Reality

"A simple, but powerful book. *Using Values to turn Vision into Reality* can help you and everyone in your organization live by your vision. Read it!"

Ken Blanchard, Co-author of The One Minute Manager

"Refreshing and useful. Effectively takes important leadership concepts and brings them to life."

Peggy Williams, President, Ithaca College